A HISTORY OF
TYLDESLEY

John Lunn
Edited by Peter Riley

P & D Riley

First Published 1953
By Tyldesley Urban District Council

This Edited Edition First Published 1995
By P & D Riley,
12 Bridgeway East,
Runcorn,
Cheshire,
England.

ISBN: 1 874712 07 7

Typography & this edition copyright © by P & D Riley

British Library Cataloguing - in - Publication Data
A Catalogue Record for this Book is available from the British Library.

Printed & Bound in England

Original Preface

THIS new History of Tyldesley has been prepared at the request of the Urban District Council of Tyldesley and is published to commemorate the Coronation of Her Most Gracious Majesty, Queen Elizabeth II.

The Council wishes to place on record its appreciation of the public service to the community rendered by the author—John Lunn, M.A., Ph.D. (Cantab.), M.Ed., LL.B. (Manchester), and to thank him for the great amount of research which has been carried out by him in preparing this book, all this work having been done entirely free of any charge to the Council.

To the many ladies and gentlemen, organisations and associations who have afforded unlimited facilities for research, the Council also express their thanks.

The thanks of the Council are also due to those ladies and gentlemen, organisations, etc., who have given financial support to the publication of this History of Tyldesley.

To all those who love this town of Tyldesley and who have had associations or connections with the township, the Council commend this book, which they feel sure will be found of interest.

FOREWORD

By SIR C. H. SHAKERLEY, BT., D.L.

—◄•■•►—

I have been requested by the Tyldesley Urban District Council to write a foreword to Mr. Lunn's historical account of the Township of Tyldesley-cum-Shakerley.

Many local histories are, except perhaps to antiquarians, somewhat heavy reading; but I am sure every reader will find these pages of absorbing interest. To me, at least, this is a fascinating account of the development and continuity of English Civic life from the earliest days. I am glad to see that though, in the Middle Ages, some of my ancestors were not of exemplary character; their contemporaries, the Tyldesleys, were even wilder !

I congratulate the civic authorities of Tyldesley on a most original enterprise; and also Mr. John Lunn, on a scholarly and interesting History, which shows the marks of many hours of devoted research.

CYRIL H. SHAKERLEY.

Editor's Note

In 1953 John Lunn published his book 'A History of Tyldesley' through the good offices of Tyldesley Urban Distrivt Council who had long sought to have a comprehensive history of the town available for sale. The work was written by Mr Lunn, a prolific researcher and local history writer, who was later to produce an equally sought after history of the neighbouring towns of Leigh, Atherton and Astley.

In the past couple of years I have had the pleasure of editing Mr Lunn's original books on Leigh and Atherton for consumption by an insatiable public, who have also asked me many times since if Lunn's book on Tyldesley was going to be republished, and after much consideration it has been decided to do just that. Here is the result!

Mr Lunn, despite his obsession with his subject, still made mistakes (who doesn't?), and it has been pointed out that a number of errors came to light in his previous books. If that is the case in this book then I am sure observant readers in the area will soon let me know. I hope they do, for in the event of a further reprint of this book, it will then be possible to correct any mistakes through footnotes.

As with the history of Leigh and Atherton, it is regrettable that the original work has had to be edited, but with rising printing costs forcing cover prices ever higher, the only way to produce a book which stays within the pocket of almost everyone is to reduce the number of pages, and this, without exception, is a very difficult decision to make. How do you edit out what maybe important to one family or some readers? How do you make that decision, necessary though it is, that may upset the ancestors of some of the people in Lunn's book? It is an answer I cannot give other than by saying "by instinct" coupled with a historian's judgement. I hope I have made the right decision and readers will enjoy this book!

PETER RILEY, 1995.

Acknowledgements

The publishers would like to thank the following for their help in the preparation of this book.

Florence Baxter
Dawn French
Tony Ashcroft

A SHORT HISTORY OF THE TOWNSHIP OF TYLDESLEY

The Roman Road, c. 200 A.D.

The area occupied by the township of Tyldesley to-day was in Roman times part of the territory of the Brigantes. The location was important, for the site lay in the triangle marked by the military stations of Manchester, Warrington, and Wigan. A Roman road ran through Tyldesley and was traceable a hundred years ago just south of Keeper Delph, where it went in a direct course north west and crossed Mort Lane just below the site of Great Boys pit. Then it curved direct west north of Cleworth Hall and was lost again just south of Shakerley Old Hall. The siting of these two ancient homes appears to have been made more in relation to the convenience offered by the Roman road rather than by that of the main highway of Sale Lane and Elliott Street. Plotting the direct course of the Roman road south west, it leads across the boundary brook at a point midway between the Delph and Ellenbrook Chapel.

The Two Amphorae

In the year 1947 two gardeners, George Bailey and Alfred Grundy, were digging in the Delph not far distant from this ancient road, when they uncovered a flag beneath which were two urns, set about the depth of a foot. The amphorae contained about 600 Roman coins.

The Coins of Postumus, Victorinus, and Tetricus

The bronze coins were minted by four emperors. The earliest are those of Postumus, who as Governor of Gaul under Valerian made himself puppet emperor in 259 A.D. He was followed by his general Victorinus, who ruled in Gaul and Britain until his assassination in 270 A.D. Then Tetricus succeeded: he gave his namesake son the rank of Caesar and both abdicated in 273 A.D. This Roman coinage, which was silver plated originated in Gaul and passed over in trade to these islands.

The Candle of History, 200-1200 A.D.

After the disclosure of the Roman urns, there is nothing for 1,000 years to trace out the steps of destiny in these parts. Everything is blank and dark. The candle of history lit by the Roman-Celts flickers out until the scribes of Cockersand Abbey in north Lancashire relight it in the reign of King John. When the shadows begin to retreat there is seen in existence a church at Leigh and a parish; within that parish is the township of Tyldesley; there are people and manors, landmarks and a new order of things, and from that time the established history of Tyldesley runs on afresh.

The Early Landscape

The Tyldesley deeds, which have survived, show by their topo-graphical names, a landscape much different from that which the generations of this century and last have imposed upon the banks and which to-day is so familiar. In the 13th and 14th c. there were dense forests in all parts of Tyldesley. Higher Oak and Lower Oak are to-day faint echoes of these woodlands, as was the Hurst, the old name for Mosley Common. A Clowes deed of 1301 tells of the Woodfall, and the same record gives other place names in which sike is a compound. This word of Norse origin meant a small brook running as a ditch on boggy land and which was so shallow as to dry up in summer. Fruyndessyke and Solyneshurstsyche were once well known, though to-day their identification is conjectural. Adam Tyldesley's lease of 1307 is evidence of the desire of the land holding classes to get their farms cleared of green and dead wood and to make pastures of this assarted area. When the Banks had been deforested, a word of Norse origin creeps in. This was brisk, a term applied to a hillside cleared of growth. These old descriptions betray the presence of a certain Norse element mixing with that Saxon population, which gave the township its name and which carefully prescribed its boundaries. Both Tyldesley and Shakerley are Saxon. The charters of Cockersand Abbey perpetuate other place names—Hollowoak, Knottyoak, Blackleach, Blacksike, Blacklowbrook, Hollowsike, Five Oaks, and Hayleycombe. There was a brook so well known that it was used as a boundary mark in many deeds and which is pure Saxon. It was called Goderic brook. The Heywood deeds disclose other names—Cartleach, Fairhurst, Witchbrook, Herberdisclogh, Aldussike, Hendam, and Colloeyssiche, localities identifiable by the men and women of the 14th c. A Hulton deed of 1347 tells of Gromhurst in Tyldesley. But few traces of Norman influence have lived on. Great Boys and the traditional pronunciation of Banks are two isolated survivals affixed to-day to the modern scene. The deeds show a township which for many ages was densely forested, chiefly with oaks; the land well watered with brooks and rills and on the plain south of the banks patches of mossland and waste.

The Vill of Tyldesley

Tyldesley was one of the six vills or townships which made up that ancient ecclesiastical unit—the parish of Leigh. The townships came before the parish and of these Pennington and Atherton were the first. The area assigned to Tyldesley was the largest; it covers some 2,610 statute acres. The local government unit of the vill was the manor; the lord of the manor performed a variety of duties. Over the manor was a chief manor; for Tyldesley this was Warrington and at the Court Leet at Warrington were elected or arbitrarily

8

chosen the various officers required to carry out the duties of township government. Besides this feudal direction, there was the royal jurisdiction acting in concurrence. The vill of Tyldesley was for this purpose in the hundred of West Derby and royal officers, sheriff, undersheriff, coroner, bailiff, and others acted mainly in the maintenance of law and justice within the hundred. Supplementing these two was the church government, which for Tyldesley was fixed on Chester, first as the archidiaconal and later as the diocesan centre with Warrington as the head of the deanery. This church jurisdiction was exercised through the parish church at Leigh and concerned itself with morals, wills, collection of tithes and dues, and minor matters such as declarations as to marriage, legitimacy, and solemn acts of publication.

The Manor of Tyldesley

The early manor of Tyldesley was Astley Hall, which explains why to-day the manor of Astley lies within the Tyldesley township boundary. The Great Inquest of 1212 shows Hugh Tyldesley as owing homage to the fief of Widnes as well as to the fief of Warrington. Astley township never in its long history came under the feudal power of Warrington. In 1301 Henry Tyldesley divided his extensive lands and a new manor was set up for Tyldesley, which owed service to the Botelers at Warrington. The two vills of Astley and Tyldesley thenceforth developed their own manorial history. For a long number of years no distinctive name was applied to the manor of Tyldesley; then later it acquired the name of Nicholas Manor and the first time that Garratt occurs is in 1505 in the homage roll of Warrington, when John Tyldesley swore fealty in the Hall at Bewsey for his lands at Garratt. Afterwards to the present time this name is both general and affixed. But a manor was sometimes an abstraction of rights and when in 1331 Thurstan Tyldesley was married to Margaret Worsley of Wardley Hall certain rights and lands, part of the manor of Tyldesley were detached and transferred to Wardley. Ultimately neighbouring halls rose into prominence and were styled manors. Their owners acquired by purchase some of the ancient manorial rights. Shakerley Old Hall and Chaddock were not original manors, but later became manors by reputation.

The Tyldesley Family

This great and noble lineage was first nurtured on the Banks. As time wore on, it was allied by marriage and purchase to other localities. In the 16th and 17th c. the family attained county status. Besides Tyldesley they acquired by marriage in 1331 Wardley Hall; by marriage again in 1560 Morley Hall. After the Reformation, when they refused to change their faith, the family migrated for reasons of seclusion to North Lancashire. The records show them as having at one time or other possessed land or rights in Tyldesley, Astley,

Swinton, Westwood, Haughton, Hulton, Culcheth, Euxton, Liverpool, Warrington, Manchester, Ditton, Pilling, Blackpool, Stalmine, Entwisle, Wyresdale, Kenyon, Arrowe in Cheshire, and Barnston in Buckinghamshire.

Hugh the Pious

Hugh Tyldesley is the second known to posterity of this glorious line. He was son to Henry. He was piously disposed towards the church and in his lifetime he endowed the monastic house of Cockersand in north Lancashire with extensive grants from his lands in both Astley and Tyldesley. Hugh gave to the canons the whole of the hamlet of Shakerley and his deed in patent form ran: " Know all men future as well present that I Hugh Tyldesley give and grant and by this present charter confirm to the house of the Blessed Mary of Cockersand and the brothers there serving God a certain parcel of my land in Tyldesley, that is to say, Shakerley, within these boundaries, from the head of the hedge in the east following Shakerley brook as far as the boundary of Hollowoak where the cross stands, from Hollowoak to the road and following the road to the boundary of Knottyoak and from Knottyoak to Blackleach and from Blackleach following the middle of the Moss even to the head of the aforesaid hedge To hold in pure and perpetual gift, freely and equally from all service of reaping and pannage to the said brothers for the good of my soul, of that of my wife, my ancestors and successors this gift I warrant to the aforesaid brothers against all men for ever. Witnesses: Richard Worsley, William Radcliff, Ithel Hulton, Richard le clerk of Fishwick, Robert Hulton, Hugh Winwick."

The date of this deed is in the early years of the 13th c. Pious Hugh died sometime after 1226 and was succeeded by his son Henry, who in 1242 paid Gascon scutage on his lands in Tyldesley.

The Hamlet of Chaddock

In the middle ages men spoke of Chaddock as a hamlet; for a small number of houses clustered round the venerable hall, which became and was for a long period the central hearth of this little hamlet. At one time it looked as if the name of Chaddock would grow and designate a thriving community with interests peculiar to itself within the eastern part of Tyldesley. Such was not to be; the name yielded to the more common adoption of Booths, a neighbouring hall and in the end Boothstown became general. Chaddock declined and the name to-day is attached merely to the hall and to a part of the highway, which provides access for it to the outside world. The origin of Chaddock has perplexed many minds; the common spelling in medieval times was Chaydock, representing the leisured drawl of those days. Then the vowel became short and the sequent consonant doubled. The last component is undoubtedly oak.

Abbot Thomas of Cockersand

Hugh the Pious gave Shakerley to the premonstratensian canons of Cockersand and henceforth to the Reformation, the holders of Shakerley paid rent and dues to the conventual bursar. Sometime during the course of the 13th c. Thomas, Abbot of Cockersand confirmed Robert Shakerley in his possession of the hamlet. Then after the death of Abbot Thomas, Adam, Robert's son made acknowledgment to the abbey and his deed has survived. The rent reserved was 12d. per annum and this sum continued to be paid to the year of the Dissolution. Many Shakerleys appear in the quittance rolls of the monastery year after year paying the old reservation in spite of the continued depreciation in the value of money.

Adam Shakerley Pays a Rent of Two White Gloves

Besides the canons of Cockersand the Shakerleys paid acknowledgment dues to the Tyldesleys. This was to safeguard the feudal rights of the local manor over all free tenants within the township. Adam, when he made his confirmation held besides Shakerley, Fiveacreshurst and Ylgrudig and for these estates he paid yearly to Adam Tyldesley one pair of white gloves at the feast of Easter.

Le Machons Landes

Sometime during the early 14th c. Makants first leaps into the floodlight of recorded documents. Adam was tenant at this time. The deeds are:

Know all men that I Adam Tyldesley son of Henry Tyldesley have given to Adam le Mason of Tyldesley and his heirs a certain part of my arable land, woods and meadows in the town of Tyldesley. Witnesses: William Atherton, Richard Hulton, Adam Bradshaw, Roger Bradshaw, Ralph Overton, clerk and others.

To all men Adam Tyldesley sends greetings in the Lord. Know ye that I have leased to Adam le Machonn and his wife and his sons a piece of land belonging to me in Tyldesley for a term of 16 years from the feast of St. Martin in the first year of King Edward the Second. Witnesses: Hugh Bradshaw, John Harper, Roger Bradshaw, Roger son of Anneis and others.

The name Makants was pronounced soft at this period. Later the " c " hardened. The rent reserved was evidently 6s. 8d. per annum for among the Shakerley deeds there is a receipt of Adam Tyldesley from Adam Mason for that amount in the year 1312. Later in 1315 Henry Shakerley released to Adam Mason and his heirs all his rights and claim in the lands and houses of Makants.

From Adam the tenancy eventually fell to Henry le Machon, whose wife was Agnes. In 1371 the widow surrendered all her dower right to her son Adam. In 1391 Henry Tyldesley leased lands in Tyldesley to Henry le Mason, which had been formerly granted to Adam the clerk and William his son. Then in 1402 comes the first recorded settlement of Makants. It was made by Agnes le Machon to Hugh son of Adam le Machon and his heirs, in default to Alice Bradshaw her daughter and heirs, remainder to the rightful heirs of Agnes. This Adam was living in 1432, for he conveyed his lands in Tyldesley to Simon Astley, who in 1450 reconveyed them to Geoffrey Shakerley the elder. Shakerley sold them in 1459 to Gilbert Urmston and the estate in this deed is styled le Machons landes. But the Makants still lived on at the yeoman house in Mort Lane; many of their stolid family were registered at Leigh where the name is spelt variantly, Maconde, Makant. Randulf was tenant in 1572 and Adam, who had £4. 6s. 8d. of goods, in 1585. In Elizabeth's reign Thurstan Tyldesley of Wardley gave licence to Thomas Fleetwood of the Peel to make a conduit through Makants lands. Randle took the oath in 1641 and Samuel in 1696. In 1838 Peter Makin was tenant of Old Hatters.

Adam Tyldesley in Lancaster Gaol, 1275

Adam had been imprisoned by the sheriff and immured at Lancaster charged with having occasioned the death of John Bradshaw. On the same charge and in prison was Alan, son of Benedict Wigan. In March, 1275, letters were dispatched to the sheriff commanding him to bail out the prisoners. This Adam was a close friend of Nicholas Wigan, rector of Leigh, who was murdered on Sunday, February 9, 1275. The rector made him an executor of his will and in 1278 Adam sought to get in debts due to the estate. Along with his co-executor he sued among others the Prior of Burscough and Roger, the dean of Warrington, for sums which they unjustly detained.

The Enfeoffment of 1301

Henry Tyldesley gave to Adam his son lands in Tyldesley in this year. The original charter was translated in the 17th c. and it is this copy which has survived. The deed gives many local landmarks. The grant was defined as beginning at a ditch on the land of Alexander Coldale, which is called the Spenne upon the south part, then following the ditch towards the moss to the hayment of Matthew Hurst, following the closes of Hurst on the north part of the Woodfall, then along the King's hedge of the Woodfall to the Fruyndesyke, then to a pit called the Kingsway and along the pit to Mosseld Yard and so on to the land of Richard Wykeshagh on the south side of the brooks. Arrived here the surveyors ascended the brooks to Solyneshurstsyke as far as the land of Margaret Wigan, sometime the wife of Walter the Fuller, across this land to the fields of Richard son of Richard son of John Hulton as far as the division of Worsley, then to the boundary of Hulton, then to Atherton and coming down to the division between Atherton and Tyldesley to the land of Adam again.

Included in the grant were the homages and services of Henry Shakerley, John Waverton, John son of Hugh Hulton, and Richard son of John Wykeshagh with all reliefs, escheats, liberties, commons, ways and gates, mills, meadows and pastures, and egress and ingress to the vill of Tyldesley. Nine witnesses attested the deed which was executed in Tyldesley on Friday before the Feast of St. Barnabas the Apostle, 1301.

Gillibrand Bank

The name Gillibrand is very old in Lancashire and in the ancient parish of Leigh especially so. This yeoman holding of 17 Cheshire acres is first betrayed by a marriage agreement made by Henry Shakerley in 1308. John Gilybront and William Gilybront were witnesses. In 1391 another William appears and in 1402 a Roger, in 1450 and 1457 Nicholas. By 1490 there is Thurstan, whose heir was William. In 1602 the occupiers of Gillibrands are styled husband-men. Richard and John Gilliborne were charged with obstructing the highway at Mosley Common called at that time " Gilliborne Bancke." There are numerous Gillibrands in the parish registers at Leigh. Thomas took the oath in 1641 and John in 1696. This John had taken his child Richard to be baptised at Leigh on November 18, 1638, and the parish clerk wrote beneath the entry a complaint that it was the fault of the parent that the entry had been misplaced. As the parent had nothing to do with the writing up of the register, the matter of fault remains obscure. By 1742 the family had lost its centuries old patrimony, for Peter Grundy and John Edge were then in joint occupation. But the name still lived on in the township and Geoffrey Gillibrand paid 4s. poor relief in that year. In 1838 Samuel Gillibrand was tenant of the Warrington School land trustees; he paid a modest rent for a cottage and a garden.

Adam Tyldesley Grants a Lease for Eleven Winters

Adam was the son of Henry, who married Hawise and succeeded his father Hugh the Pious. His lease says:

This indenture bears witness that Adam son of Henry Tyldesley leases and demises to John Leywayhe all the land which he previously held of him in the town of Tyldesley with all appurtenances to have and to hold to the aforesaid John and his wife and their heirs from the aforesaid Adam and his heirs freely and peacefully with all profits and fines appertaining to the said land, namely for a term of eleven years to be fully completed beginning at the Feast of St. Martin in the winter following the confirmation of this present writing in the year of grace 1307, rendering as rent from the afore-said John and his wife and their heirs to the aforesaid Adam and his heirs one silver mark twice per year, one half at Pentecost and one half at Martinmas, and his second best pig in lieu of pannage and if the aforesaid John has no pigs then it is testified that he will give twelve pennies in lieu of the pig for all services and exactions. And the aforesaid Adam and his heirs will guarantee all that land held by the aforesaid John and his wife against all comers and the aforesaid John and his wife or the one who lives the longer will clear before the end of the term all the green and dead wood standing on the aforesaid land and until this be done he will pay 3s. 6d. for every acre not cleared before the end of the term.

Witnesses: Henry Shakerley, John Waverton, Richard Valentine, clerk and others. Given at Tyldesley on Thursday before the Feast of St. John before the Latin Gate, 1307.

Chaddock Hall

The first recorded tenant of Chaddock was Reginald. The early Chaddock deeds were copied out by the antiquary Cuerden and these are now in the British Museum. William was the son of Reginald and he gave one half of Chaddock hamlet to Elias, son of Robert Chaddock. Hugh Tyldesley as a superior lord had to confirm this grant. He was Hugh the Pious. The same William gave Robert Chaddock one half of the estate, so that father Elias and son Robert once held the whole between them. In a confirmation grant by Henry Tyldesley, Hugh's successor, two brothers of the Chaddock family figure as witnesses, John and Thomas. Their father's name was John. The same Henry granted a piece of assart land near to Chaddock to Robert son of Elias. All these early tenants lived in the 13th c.

Cleworth Hall

Cleworth is of great antiquity and its first mention occurs in the 14th c. In 1333 it was held by William Waverton as mesne lord; it then comprised 27 acres of wood and meadow and William conveyed to Adam Chaddock a life estate with the reversion to William, his son, and his wife Margaret. The house was at that date tenanted by Richard son of Robert Cleworth. Agnes Cleworth is mentioned in 1336. An undated deed of c. 1340 tells that Roger son of Geoffrey Astley exchanged a carucate of land in Astley for " Clewod in Tyldesley " and seven acres clearly meted and William Cleworth was a witness to the charter.

The Execution on Leyland Moor, 1315

It was on Tuesday, the Feast of St. Martin, that a posse of 300 strong of the Holland faction came to Charnock Richard, and there with force and arms seized the person of two knights, Adam Banaster and Henry Lee. They led them to Leyland Moor and there beheaded them. Among those indicted for this heinous crime was Hugh Tyldesley. Adam, Henry, Robert, and John, his brothers, with Henry Hog were all retainers of the Holland confederacy. John Tyldesley and Adam were further charged with having hunted in Musbury Royal Park and the free chase of Rossendale. Sometimes these lawless sons of Hugh rode under the banner of Thurstan Norley to steal livestock and break the King's peace.

Robert Tyldesley at Warrington, 1317

Robert Tyldesley in this year, though jurors differed and some said it was 1322 or 1323, killed Adam Scott. Henry Tyldesley, his brother, and Ralph Kay aided and abetted. After the crime, Robert was harboured in shelter by his kinsman, Robert Holland. Scott was a servant of William Boteler, at his manor of Warrington.

The Burning of Wardley Hall, February 21, 1317

On this date, Monday in the first week of Lent 10, Edward II, the Tyldesley brothers, Hugh, Henry, Adam, and Robert, sons of Hugh burned down Wardley Hall, the house of Margaret Worsley, and killed Robert, son of Martin the clerk, whose body they threw into the flames. After the felony their father harboured them. The sheriff was ordered to arrest them, but he was able to seize only Hugh; the others fled and he was commanded to cause the culprits to be exacted from county court to county court and if they did not appear to outlaw them. Later, Robert Holland paid £10 to Margaret to induce her not to sue at law the Tyldesley brothers and so to hide the felony.

Assault at Preston, 1319

The brothers Henry, Robert, John, Adam, and Hugh were all together at Preston about this year. While there, on Sunday the Feast day of St. Wilfrid, October 14, they entered the house of Aubrey, son of Adam Preston: they thrashed, wounded and maimed him. In the indictment they were all stigmatised as common evil-doers.

The Battle of Chaddock Hurst, December 8, 1321

In the early 14th c. Henry Chaddock and Katherine his wife are mentioned in a grant. The subsidy roll of 1332 shows Henry and Adam in possession. Both tenants paid 12d. tax on their moveable property and evidently the Hall was still divided, as it had been in the earlier century. The area round the old mansion was thickly wooded and the name Chaddock Hurst was the name used to distinguish the Chaddock estate from the fields and forest lands of the Tyldesleys to the north known then as Tyldesleyhurst.

It was here on December 8, 1321, that the din and clangour of battle was heard. Two rival confederate groups of the Earl of Lancaster met together, the Hindleys and the Tyldesleys, numbering 80 men on one side and 50 on the other. In this affray four of the Tyldesley supporters, Adam Tyldesley, Jordan Carrington, Richard Strongbow, and Robert Barton were killed. Adam was the son of Hugh Tyldesley.

The Attack on Blackrod Manor, 1323

On Sunday after St. Paul's Conversion in January of this year a large force of tumultuous men assembled under Robert Holland and marched to the manor of Blackrod, which was the property of William Bradshaw. Their intent was to burn the house down and in the company of the marauders was Hugh, son of Hugh Tyldesley. Arrived there, they found the manor defended by Bradshaw and his adherents, who shot out arrows at the assailing force. Richard Boteler and Richard Wade were both killed.

Hugh Tyldesley Stands Mute of Malice, 1323

The Sheriff brought Hugh to stand his trial before the King, Edward of Carnarvon, at Wigan in the last months of 1323. When arraigned and charged Hugh stood mute of malice and as he refused to plead, he was sent back to prison. The entry on the roll reads: Hugh son of Hugh Tyldesley was arrested for the destruction of the house of Margaret Worsley at Worsley by fire and for the death of Robert son of Martin the clerk whom he and others killed and whose body they cast into the fire, so that it was burned with the house; also for the death of John Bickerton, servant of William Bradshaw, who was killed at Leyland church; and for the theft of a palfrey from Thomas Banaster. On interrogation he feigns dumbness, but a jury of inquisition declares that he can speak if he will and has spoken that present day. He is therefore sent back to prison for a day.

Hugh had to remain in confinement under the close watch of the King's Marshal Eudo de Walle.

Another entry on the rolls of assize said that Adam, Robert, John, and William, brothers to Hugh, along with Henry Hog of Tyldesley, were implicated in the death of Bickerton, as well as the theft of the palfrey.

The sheriff had great difficulty in bringing their bodies to court; sometimes it was reported that Hugh, son of Hugh Tyldesley, was dead and that the others could not be found and had nothing by which they could be attached. Later, Hugh was declared guilty of the charges preferred against him and he was fined £20. His sureties, Robert Wilkshaw, Adam Gregory, William Gillibrand senior and Henry Chaddock were all men of the vill of Tyldesley.

Isabella Tyldesley at Westminster, 1324

Isabella was the widow of Henry Tyldesley. Her husband being dead and the heir Adam, son of Adam Tyldesley, was under age. The custody of the lands and heir went to John Chisenhall of Longshaw and until Adam attained his majority, Chisenhall would take the profits. Isabella claimed her dower third and the custodee refused to acknowledge her right. The estate comprised six messuages, one water mill, 90 acres of land, 10 of meadow, 40 of wood, 30 of pasture, and 40s. rent, all in Tyldesley. To claim her right Isabella undertook the perilous journey to London and appeared at Westminster before the King's Court in the Trinity term of 1324. Chisenhall did not come and the court clerk wrote on the roll: " It is considered that he wage the law with her with the twelfth hand and let him come with his law in the quindene of St. Michael."

The Abduction of November 7, 1331

Jordan Worsley, lord of Wardley, had died and left an only heiress Margaret. Her marriage was eagerly coveted in the neighbourhood and on Wednesday after the feast of the Circumcision, 1331, Richard Tyldesley came to an agreement with John Shirburn and Agnes his wife, by which was conceded to Richard the custody and the right of marriage of the young Margaret. The Shirburns evidently had this feudal power, which they negotiated to the Tyldesleys. Margaret's kinsman, Richard Worsley refused to give up the child. Henry the Malefactor on Thursday after the feast of St. Leonard went to Wardley, took the girl away and married her to his son Thurstan. This marriage proved of historic import, for the Tyldesleys thereby became possessed of Wardley and a new branch and house of their family was founded. They held Wardley to the year 1582. Thurstan received a grant of part of the manorial rights of Tyldesley manor, which explains why certain old quit rents in the eastern part of Tyldesley were payable to Wardley. Margaret was of tender age at this date: she was living in 1410, 79 years after the abduction. She became the mother of Thomas, the sergeant-at-law and of Hugh, retainer of the Earl of Gloucester.

Adam Tyldesley Impleads Hugh the Elder, 1332

At the Feast of St. Peter's Chains, 1332, Adam Tyldesley and his wife Agnes complained that Hugh Tyldesley the elder had withheld a rent of two marks and had dispossessed them of a free tenement in Tyldesley. Adam came to court and brought the charter deed, which Hugh the elder had executed. He produced it to support his claim. Hugh did not come, although he had sureties in Henry del Hurst and Richard Hert. The judge ordered a local view to be taken and after the enquiry, it was reported to the court that Adam and Agnes had been turned out. Hugh was ordered to pay them 16s. 8d. damages and he was put at the mercy of the court. Adam later became the Cain of the family of Tyldesley.

The Tyldesley Brothers before King Edward III, June, 1335

The Tyldesley brothers—les freres Tyldesley—sons of Hugh, those notorious trespassers against the royal peace, rode commonly to churches, fairs and markets to the terror of the people and robbed them; they were the lawless highwaymen and bandits of this reign. By June the sheriff had managed to get hold of their bodies and they were brought before the king at Westminster. There was Adam with his brothers, John, Robert, and William; there was a namesake Adam, son of Adam Tyldesley, and Henry his brother, and 13 others charged in the indictment. They were all found guilty and committed to the prison of the Marshalsea. At the foot of the engrossed entry on the Coram Rege Roll was added afterwards: " Adam paid a fine, as appears by the roll of fines of this term."

Henry the Malefactor

Henry Tyldesley was one of the many sons of Hugh, and like his father was patriarch of a numerous issue. His lands were styled the Hurst and he was known sometimes as de Tyldesleyhurst. He paid 2s. 8d. tax in 1332. His wife's name was Alice and by 1357 he had died. He was a notorious trespasser against the royal peace. In 1341 on Sunday night before the feast of St. Gregory he broke into several houses and beat the inmates. Three years later the Grand Inquisition presented to the royal justices in eyre a long list of his known misdeeds. He had taken a bribe from William Penke, whom he had arrested as a robber and had set him free; he had shot at William son of Adam Bradshaw and demolished his house at Aspull; he had chased Henry de Trafford and his relatives from Tyldesley to Atherton and had hamstrung Robert son of John de Trafford. In Tyldesley he possessed a stronghold known as " la Pele " and there he immured his victims. He had wounded William Anderton at Wigan and had broken into the corn mills there taking 10 quarters of tollcorn worth 20s. He had forced entry into the house of John son of Richard Wigan and had drawn blood from Richard son of Adam de Trafford. He was known to the justices as a common evil-doer and a leader of people in the markets and fairs against the peace of the Lord king. At Pentecost in 1343 at Tyldesley he had killed two steers belonging to Adam Hulton and had wounded 12 oxen and heifers in Adam's close. He tore down the fences of Roger Hulton and damaged his fields and ditches. The justices fined him and sent him to gaol. In 1325 along with his brothers John and Robert he had been outlawed for his many felonies. The sheriff could not find them to bring them to justice and Robert Woodhouse, keeper of the wardrobe was ordered to search his rolls and certify the court whether or no they were in any army on service beyond the seas in Gascony. Henry took part in the Liverpool riots against the king's judges; he opposed Blewbury, rector of Leigh and in 1331, 1335, and 1336 paid fines to him. In 1348 he took a grant of eight acres in the Park at Tyldesley along with his wife, with turbary for one mansion and liberty to dig in the land. In 1345 he was appointed a recognitor and because he disobeyed the summons was fined. Before 1357 he was dead, for in that year his widow Alice appears in a plea of dower.

Tyldesley in 1377

About this time the townships of the ancient parish of Leigh were assessed to pay a subsidy to the King. Tyldesley paid 25s., Astley 20s., and Atherton 35s. The list for Tyldesley gives the following contributors:

Vill de Tyldesley

Richard, son of Adam Tyldesley.	John Throstell and his wife.
Richard Turnour.	Adam Soler ,, ,, ,,
Peter Shakerley.	Hugh Wilkshaw ,, ,, ,,
Thurstan Layland.	Robert Layland ,, ,, ,,
Hugh Pull.	John Hilton ,, ,, ,,
John Wood.	Richard Birchall ,, ,, ,,
Richard Croft.	Richard Woodward.
John Topping.	John Marshall.

Total 25s.

Medieval Yeomen

Three families of Tyldesley yeomen occur with frequency on the records; they were the substantial land-tilling class which formed the backbone of society in England at that time. In Tyldesley the families were the Wilkshaws, the Laylands, and the Gregorys. Robert Wilkshaw was a surety of the Hugh Tyldesley, who stood mute of malice. This was in 1323; probably it was the same Robert and Agnes his wife who in 1348 trespassed on Adam Tyldesley's field. In 1356 John Wilkshaw's daughter Margery was a plaintiff and in 1377 there is Hugh Wilkshaw, whose wife was Alice, according to a law case in 1375. Robert Layland was a tenant in Shakerley; he had died by 1333, when Lora, his widow, claimed against Henry Shakerley and Agnes, his lady, a life interest in four houses and five acres. John was son and heir of Robert. In 1375 Robert Layland paid his bribe to the wapentake bailiff and in 1377 he appeared along with Thurstan Layland. Adam Gregory was a surety for the evil Hugh in 1323; Hugh Gregory occurs in 1352 and in 1375 Robert Gregory. Robert was son of Hugh and at Tyldesley on Wednesday in the octave of the Annunciation of the Virgin, 1363, he conveyed his rights in certain lands in the hamlet of Chaddock to Gilbert, son of Hugh Whynlegh.

Chaddock in the 14th Century

Adam Chaddock, the taxpayer of 1332, in the next year took a lease of Cleworth Hall from William Waverton. Adam was an opponent of Blewbury, rector of Leigh, and paid over fines to him. In 1350 the Chaddock lands were valued at 40d., and Thomas, son of John, was the tenant. This Thomas had taken part in the Liverpool riots in 1346. The Chaddocks were just as turbulent and lawless as their more powerful neighbours, the Tyldesleys. A deed of later years of the 14th c. shows Henry, son of Thomas Chaddock, confirming a grant to his mother Alice of certain lands in the hamlet of Chaddock. These were the fields and tenements in the occupation of Matilda, widow of William Tumcookson. The land possessed common of pasture, estover rights, and other easements.

The Archers of Chaddock Hall

The tenants of the Tyldesley, Shakerley, and Chaddock lands were often summoned to do military service. In 1360 the retinue roll of the King shows William Chaddock as an archer on foot. He was noted in the roll as *potens de corpore et bonis* or fit for active service in both body and accoutrements. A later muster roll of John Stanley informs posterity that Hugh Tyldesley was an archer on horseback. Hugh Chaddock and Richard Tyldesley were foot archers, serving under Herford, captain. They all drew daily pay for service from July 22 to October 21 of the year 1391.

Agnes Sunderland at Cripplegate, 1399

Agnes possessed certain lands and houses in the hamlet of Chaddock in the town of Tyldesley. In 1376, by a deed dated at Cripplegate, Friday after the Feast of St. Michael, she quitclaimed to Thomas Tyldesley, son of Thurstan, all her rights in the aforesaid property. This Thomas had evidently met Agnes in London. He was the famous sergeant-at-law and it was by his influence that an entry of Agnes' warranty to him of her estate was eventually engrossed upon the Close Rolls of the King. In 1410 Thomas charged his executors to agree with the heir of Agnes about these lands in Chaddock "and this quickly, as they will answer to me before the supreme judge." Agnes died before Thomas: he paid for masses for her soul.

Hugh Tyldesley, Retainer of the Earl of Gloucester, 1400

Hugh was in the service of Thomas le Despenser, Earl of Gloucester. It is said that he was clerk of the kitchen. Gloucester had accompanied King Richard II to Ireland, but on his downfall he deserted this hapless monarch. Soon after, Despenser conspired against Henry IV, but the citizens of Bristol seized his person and beheaded it at the High Cross. He was attainted of high treason and all his lands were confiscated. Gloucester had on October 1, 1399, granted to Hugh a yearly pension of 10 marks issuing out of the profits of the manor of Kimberworth in Yorkshire. Tyldesley was cautious and suspicious of the political end of his patron and next day he made over the pension to four trustees, one of whom was his brother Thomas, the sergeant-at-law. Later, in December. 1400, Tyldesley was one of the many petitioners seeking to protect their rights in various manors in Buckinghamshire, Wiltshire, and Southampton, which had been declared sequestrate after the death of the Earl. Hugh, who succeeded to the estate of his brother Thomas the sergeant, died in 1436, possessed of the manor of Tyldesley, New Hall, and other lands in Tyldesley, Astley, Wardley. Salford, and Mosley Hey. His eldest son, then aged 12 and named Thurstan, claimed the manor.

Nicholas Tyldesley, Parson of Prestwich, 1402

Nicholas was one of the several of the famous line who entered the church. On March 18, 1402, he was instituted to the rectory of Prestwich, near Manchester, on the presentation of King Henry 'V. He is described as a clerk and he was still at Prestwich in 1413. For on March 20 of that year Hugh, son of Thurstan Tyldesley, granted Hazelhurst in Worsley to Nicholas Tyldesley of Prestwich, Roger Bolton, John Worsley senior, and Hugh, son of Alexander Tyldesley. He had died before February, 1427; for there was at that time pending an enquiry into his estate, whereby it was disclosed that he had an interest in 30 acres of land in Manchester held of the King as Duke of Lancaster.

John Tyldesley takes the Castle and Isle of Man, 1405

The usurpation by the Lancastrian Henry IV of the throne and crown brought the Tyldesley family many advances in fortune. Favours were showered on Christopher, Thomas, and Hugh. In 1406 Hugh had been named one of the receivers of the temporalities of the archbishopric of York. He figures on the patent rolls as engaged in many dealings with important manors. Another member of the family who was entrusted with weighty missions was John. In 1405 the King sent him to the Isle of Man to take both the castle and the island into royal hands. For it was then of great strategic importance, an inviting stepping stone for any rebel insurgents coming from or crossing to the safety offered by the hostility of Ireland.

Thomas Tyldesley, Sergeant-at-Law.

Thomas was the son of Thurstan and Margaret. He went to London and there found fortune. He took to the study and practice of the law and became a member of Gray's Inn. He rose to be sergeant-at-law and was entrusted with many important missions by the Lancastrian Henry IV. He is mentioned in 1374 and was accorded royal protection in that year. Gilbert Barton of Rydale had sued both father and son for £2,000 debt. Next year both Thomas and Thurstan charged Hugh Wilkshaw and Alice Hulton with having depastured their corn and grass at Tyldesley. Another case shows that these Tyldesleys had estates at Euxton, for in 1376 Thurstan, Thomas and Joan his wife, contested eight acres of land with certain defendants. From about this time Thomas was continuously in London; in 1384 he appears, from a writ directed to the sheriff of the city, as a guarantor. Earlier in 1375 he had acquired lands in Chaddock hamlet from Agnes Sunderland and in the same year he acknowledged a debt of 40s. to Richard Farington, a clerk. In 1399 he was pleading before Gascoigne, in litigation concerning the manor of Horsham in Surrey. With the deposition of King Richard II, Thomas rose into greater prominence. For in March, 1402, he is styled a justice of assize, when his commission was joined with that of William Gascoigne. Next year he was deputed to repair the walls and ditches of the Thames to control flooding. Then on June 14, 1404, Tyldesley led for the Crown in a claim for the manor of Farndown by Byfield in Northamptonshire, and on May 18, 1409, he joined a bench of four judges and two other sergeants to settle a dispute in the Chancery at Westminster. In 1405 he was again entrusted with the repair of the Thames embankments between London Bridge and Greenwich. Other commissions rapidly followed, generally issued to himself and Sir William Gascoigne and these testify to the confidence King Henry placed in him. Tyldesley was a justice of the peace for Cumberland, Northumberland, Westmorland, all the ridings of Yorkshire, the liberty of Ripon and the town and liberty of Beverley. The picture formed of him by his will is one of a propertied London citizen, well-to-do, head of an ample household, proud, prosperous, pious, grateful for his parentage, living on terms of easy approachability with the illustrious of his day.

John Haverbergh's Cup, 1410

John Haverbergh was rector of Leigh from 1366-82; he was non-resident. Thomas Tyldesley, the sergeant-at-law knew him well; it could be, by straining the surviving evidence, that the young law student coming from Lancashire sought out this clerk by letters of commendation and was befriended by him in London. Haverbergh died in a village outside the city in 1382 and 28 years later, when Thomas was making his will, he remembered him with thankfulness. He set aside a money payment for a chaplain to say masses in the parish church at Leigh for the soul of John de Haverbergh, formerly rector. The young Thomas had in 1382 bought from the rector's executors a silver cup to be mindful of him. This was sold in 1410 and the money used for additional masses for John's departed soul.

The King to Sir William Gascoigne

Gascoigne was the friend of Thomas Tyldesley. Two writs of great significance were addressed to him by the King in the matter of the Tyldesley-Hulton feud. The first was dated July 8, 1411, and directed to Gascoigne as Chancellor of the Palatine of Lancaster; it stated that John, son of John Tyldesley, had appeared before Thomas Pinchbeck, justice, against Roger Hulton and Roger his son, and Adam, brother of Roger son of Roger, William son of Adam

Hulton, Adam Bradshaw, Henry Ballesden, and Roger Greenhalgh in the matter of the Tyldesley lands, and that the case had been transferred to Westminster.

The second writ is dated February 7, 1413. It ran as follows: " Whereas a manifest error in the assize of novel disseisin had occurred before Thomas Pinchbeck and his fellows, late justices of our Father John, Duke of Lancaster in the dispute of John son of John Tyldesley against Roger Hulton, Roger his son, now dead, Adam brother of the said Roger son of Roger, William son of Adam Hulton, Henry Ballesden, now dead, as it is said, Adam Bradshaw, Roger Greenhalgh, now dead, about certain tenements in Tyldesley to the grave damage of the said Adam, brother of Roger, son and heir of the said Roger Hulton, we therefore command you to inspect the record and do swift and full justice. Witness ourselves at Westminster, February 7, in the 14th year of our reign."

The Tyldesleys had secured a judgment in their favour and the Hultons had appealed to the King. Gascoigne lost no time in inspecting the Pinchbeck roll and bringing the parties before him.

Jack of Tyldesley, 1410

Thomas, the great sergeant, had taken into his service a youth from Tyldesley: his name was John Boys, but by his master he was known as " young Jakke of Tyldesley." As a legacy he got 100s. to bind himself as apprentice to a good and honest trade in London.

Henry Parr, 1429

The Parr family, whose name is still part of local geography, were like the Wilkshaws, Laylands, and Gregorys, yeomen in the middle ages. Their names often occur in the old records. In 1428 Oliver and Henry Parr gave up a life lease in certain lands to Thomas Chaddock. The next year the same Henry impleaded in the Duchy Court Robert Shakerley, Geoffrey, his son, the coal stealers, and Henry and James Bradshaw, sons of Ralph, from Hindley, who had thrashed him at Shakerley with intent to beat the life out of him. He said these men waylaid him there and grossly maltreated him.

Shakerley Sea-coal, 1429

In 1429 men were getting coal in Shakerley hamlet. There was a dispute between the Tyldesleys and the Shakerleys, for Hugh Tyldesley, brother of the sergeant-at-law moved in that year against Robert Shakerley, Geoffrey his son, Geoffrey Shakerley and Margaret, widow of Peter, Henry son of Ralph Bradshaw of Hindley, and James son of Ralph Bradshaw, yeomen in a plea of trespass. Hugh's complaint was that these had with a number of armed men and other malefactors dug in his soil at Tyldesley and had taken away sea-coal. The land where they had worked had been thrown up and Hugh claimed damages of 20 marks. The same Robert Shakerley and Geoffrey with others at the head of an armed multitude had waylaid Hugh at Leigh with intent to kill him and in the fight some of Hugh's servants had suffered wounds. From a grant of September 29, 1428, among the Hulton deeds it appears that Hugh's wife was named Aleson and that she had a field in Tyldesley called Tyldesleypark. In 1410 Hugh was stated to be about 40 years old. He was still living in 1436, for mention is made of him in a deed of that year.

Roger Atkinson is Distrained, 1442

The duties of a wapentake bailiff were many; he was the officer who worked closely with the sheriff, and in his perambulations of the hundred he delivered writs, arranged meeting places where official enquiries could be held, and co-ordinated the local administration under other royal officers such as the coroner. Like the higher officials he enjoyed the perquisites of office by the custom of the locality. In 1442 the bailiff of West Derby Hundred came to Tyldesley and took 7s. 6d. distress from Roger Atkinson. The sum was accounted for in due course in the Ministers' Accounts of the King. Roger lived in Shakerley and witnessed one of the Shakerley deeds in 1432.

John Tyldesley and the Manor of Tyldesley, 1469

At the Lent Session at Lancaster in 1469 John Tyldesley, senior, came to an agreement with Robert Spencer about the manor of Tyldesley. Spencer gave 20s. to the King for licence to make the agreement. It concerned three messuages, 200 acres of land, 60 of pasture, 24 of wood, 20 of meadow, and 20 of heath, all in the town of Tyldesley.

Garratt Hall in Wardship, 1509

John Tyldesley, who did homage in 1505, died on Saturday in the fifth week of Lent, 1509. At the inquisition held into his estate consequent upon his death, it was recorded that he possessed Garratt Hall, seven messuages, and 276 acres of land, meadow, pasture, and heath; the yearly rent was 20d. and there was the duty to attend the court leet every three weeks. The son and heir was Richard, then aged only eight years. The overlord of Garratt thus took the heir and lands into wardship and collected the profits of the manor. In 1511 Boteler sold the wardship and the right to marry the heir to Richard Heaton, who paid £40 for them. Heaton married the young Tyldesley to his own daughter, Mary. At the Feast of Annunciation, 1523, Tyldesley came of age. It was then said that he had been born at North Meols and had been brought up in the household of Edward Wareton.

Parnell Shakerley, c. 1510

Parnell was the local name for the Latin Petronilla. She was daughter of Geoffrey Shakerley and Anne his wife. After the dispute in 1500 she was eventually given in marriage to Thurstan Tyldesley of Wardley Hall, and her daughter in course of time married Sir Robert Worsley of Booths, whose deer the Chaddocks stole in 1547. Parnell died young, and her husband married again. Thurstan Tyldesley was in the commission of the peace for Lancashire in 1522 and one of the original feoffees of Manchester Free School in 1515.

The Constables of Tyldesley, 1516

One of the many diversified duties of the two township constables was to make the journey to Farnworth near Widnes and attend the Great Court of the West Derby Hundred there. Offences against the peace, and breaking the assize of ale and bread were frequent presentments. In 1516 Matthew Mann and John Mather, constables of Tyldesley with Shakerley were called in court, and stated that they had nothing to present. At the same great court holden in the same year on Tuesday after the Feast of Trinity the two constables did not appear, and for this neglect the whole township of Tyldesley was fined £2.

The Shakerleys Leave Shakerley Old Hall c. 1520

Geoffrey Shakerley, who had to deposit his title deeds at Manchester married for his second wife Isabel, daughter of Thomas Venables of Kinderton in Cheshire. Geoffrey was son of Peter, who had married a Cheshire heiress, Elizabeth, daughter of John Legh of Booths. Geoffrey, in 1533 at the time of Flower's Visitation of Lancashire had as issue, Peter, Robert, Thomas, Elizabeth, and Jane. From these early marriages with Cheshire heiresses flowed that association of the Shakerley family with Cheshire, and their preference for that county, whither ultimately they transferred their domicile. Geoffrey's heir was Peter, who died in 1553; his wife was Elizabeth, daughter of Sir Randal Mainwaring, and at her death in 1582 she was buried at Leigh on November 18. The next successor was Geoffrey who was sheriff of Cheshire in 1610 and who died in 1618. His wife was Jane, daughter of Sir George Beeston. Their son and heir was Peter, and he married Margaret Oldfield, who lived at Shakerley Old Hall and died there in 1667. The migration of the Shakerleys to Cheshire was a gradual process; some dowager and cadet members lived on at the Old Hall, and in 1612 Hugh Shakerley, gentleman, lived there, and was buried at Leigh in that year. But the heir ceased to be located in the hamlet, which gave his progenitors their name, and when members of the family no longer lived in the Old Hall, bailiffs were put in to manage their estates, and in the next stage of decline, the hall becomes a farmhouse.

Deer Stealers, 1547

Sir Robert Worsley kept deer at his manor of the Booths in Lostock. On June 21, 1547, there was a raid, one hour before sunrise. Thomas Chaddock, Piers Chaddock, and James Chaddock, gentlemen, with others armed with bows and bucklers stole in that park a tame deer, killed it, and carried it off to Chaddock Hall, where they consumed it.

Entwisle Manor, 1551

Thurstan Tyldesley of Wardley acquired this manor in the parish of Bolton, from George Entwisle. Thurstan settled it on his son, Edward, who married Anne Leyland of Morley Hall. The manor was kept by the Tyldesleys of Morley to the year 1670, when the piecemeal dispersion of the estate was made complete by Edmund Tyldesley.

Garratt Hall in 1558

John Tyldesley of Garratt died in this year. The jurors who enquired into his estate on October 10 swore on oath that it comprised seven messuages, 40 acres of land, 10 of meadow, 20 of pasture, six of wood, 100 of heath, and 100 of moss. The overlord was Thomas Boteler, the tenure military service, the rent 10s., the suit at the court of Warrington three weeks. The value of the manor was returned at 20 marks. Richard Tyldesley was next heir; he was John's son, aged 19 in this year.

The Shakerley Heretic, 1558

In Shakerley lived a young nailor, Jeffrey Hurst; he was the eldest of a family of twelve and had been apprenticed to the trade of nailmaking by his father. Jeffrey came under the influence of George Marsh, of Deane, who was his brother-in-law. Marsh had studied at Cambridge, and Jeffrey, by constant conversation with him became inflamed with the doctrines of Protestantism. He could read and write and was proficient in Latin. One of Hurst's most treasured possessions was William Tyndale's translation of the Bible. In time, the house of the Hursts in Shakerley became a noted hotbed of religious meetings and preachers regularly preached there.

Christmas Trees, 1605

In Garratt Hall fields, in the closes of Lambert Tyldesley, gentleman, holly grew. Ferdinando Higson, labourer, of Westleigh, entered the woods on December 26, 1605, and took away four holly trees. He assaulted John Hey. The value of the trees was assessed at 1d. each. Higson appeared in due time before the justices at quarter sessions.

Thomas Hurst, Woollen Webster, of Shakerley, 1606

The Hursts were of Shakerley. The family was very numerous and when Thomas died in October, 1606, he trusted he would be made one of the elect number to rest with Abraham, Isaac, and Jacob in the Kingdom of Heaven. Thomas owed to William Turton, his neighbour, 40s. for the rent of a piece of land, which he had taken on lease for three years. To " old Mistress Shakerley " he owed £1 13s. 4d. He directed that there was to be paid to Giles Turton 10s. " on the day of his marriage or on the day of his death, whichever doth come the sooner." His inventory drawn up on the very day of his funeral at Leigh shows a value of £40. 11s. 4d. He had cannell, coal, and turves worth 17s., linen towe and yarn 40s. 4d., and a small pair of looms with heald and other implements at 24s. His most valuable item was a lease of land from William Milliner, gentleman, which was put down at £14. He left a widow and three children, James, John, and Ann Guest. Jeffrey Hurst, the heretic, belonged to this family.

Hindsford Bridge, 1604

" Hyndforth " bridge, one end in Chowbent and the other end in Shakerley was in 1604 in great decay. It was made of wood; in 1629 the justices decided to replace this bridge by a more durable structure of stone. While the rebuilding was in progress, a petition was drawn up and signed, which stated that " at the entrance to Mosley Common " there was a bridge and that certain wooden planks of the old Hindsford Bridge could well be used to repair the Mosley Common Bridge. Among those who signed the request were Thomas Mort, of Astley, Thurstan and Hugh Parr, Ellen Chaddock of Chaddock Hall, Hugh Maken, John and Thomas Gillibrand, John Marsh, John Mather, James Wallwork, Lambert Sale, Thomas Houlden, Thomas Worsley, and Ralph Mort. From the interest shown by these signatories, the bridge was Parr Bridge.

A Loan to Nicholas Starkie, Gent., 1609

Sometimes the great folk in the halls at Tyldesley borrowed money from their humbler and thriftier tenants. Richard Battersby, nailor, lent to Geoffrey Shakerley a sum of £61 and when Margery Street, widow, died in 1610, it was learned that she had loaned £4 to Nicholas Starkie. This Nicholas was the one who was pestered with the male witch, Hartley, at Cleworth in 1696. Margery had no issue living at the date of her burial at Leigh; she left her modest competence to the six children of Ralph Mann. One of her witnesses to her will singularises himself by his unusual name; he was called Originall Flitcroft, and he came from Bedford.

Garratt Hall in 1613

Lambert Tyldesley of the Garratt died in 1613; his will has miraculously been preserved and in the inventory is mirrored a faded picture of this once great manor house. These were its rooms: kitchen, backhouse, dayhouse, mealhouse, larder, buttery, parlour, and hall. In addition there was a storehouse, closet, three chambers over the kitchen, parlour and hall, a small chamber, a servant's chamber, and a maid's room. In all these is set out and evaluated the pieces of furniture. The hall was the great room; in it was a long table, four long forms, a crooked form, and a bird case. In the closet were kept the China dishes, the Venetian glasses, the gilt salt cellar, three spoons, and a gilt plate; in the little chamber was a spinning wheel and reels. Listed in the servant's room is a cross bow, a view bow, a cocknet, and a sword. Lambert divided his goods into three shares. Two shares he gave to his well beloved wife Dorothy, but the garner in the great barn, the big iron chimney in the kitchen, and the best gilt salt cellar were to pass to his son and heir, Thomas. The remaining third share went to his two daughters, Katherine and Marie, and Dorothy, the wife, was to have the upbringing of the son Thomas, till he came of age.

A Fustian Weaver's Stock in Trade, 1613

James Partington, of Tyldesley, who was buried at Leigh on March 31, 1613, was a fustian weaver. His will is dated February 21, and on April 6 his goods and debts were drawn up for probate. Twenty customers owed him together the substantial sum of £41 12s. 8d. In fustian, single end, he had £5. 6s. 8d.; there was a pair of looms worth 8s., linen yarn 3s. 4d., wool and woollen yarn 4s., and dyed fustian 9s. He gave to Robert, his son, a keddcomb and a comb for a pair of looms " in case he shall have need of them in the Chamber in the Eastern end of the house with the license of my landlord."

Thomas Tyldesley of the Garratt at Oxford and Gray's Inn, 1614

Lambert Tyldesley who died in 1613 was buried at Leigh on March 5. On the 24 of the same month his personalty was valued. His son and heir was Thomas, who in 1614 is discovered at Oxford. He took law and entered Gray's Inn the same year. Two other members of a collateral branch of the Tyldesley family were at Oxford at the same time; they were Edward and Richard Tyldesley, who both became B.A. of University College in 1618. Their father was Sir Thomas Tyldesley, attorney-general and one of the Council of the North. He was for a time, reader at Gray's Inn. Thomas of the Garratt died in 1638.

Branches of the Tyldesley Family, 1621

Besides the Tyldesleys of Garratt, Morley, Wardley, and Peel, there were other smaller houses which appear for short periods of distinction in various parts of the realm. The Garratt House had lands at Arrowe in Cheshire, the Morley House estates at Myerscough, Stansacre, Entwisle, Blackpool, Garstang, and Holcroft, the Peel House, lands at Barnston in Buckinghamshire, and the Wardley branch, long after it had ceased to be identified with Worsley, acquired for a short time the village of Orford near Warrington. But besides these there are Tyldesleys located at Eccleshall in Staffordshire. Richard Tyldesley, S.T.B., who became Archdeacon of Rochester in 1615 belonged to this family offshoot. He died in 1621. Edmund Tyldesley was another ecclesiastical member of the same branch. Elected a fellow of Oxford in 1636, he was expelled in 1648 because of his royalist leanings. For a short time a minor family of Tyldesleys reappears in London again. Thomas Tyldesley, who attended Westminster school and who went to Trinity College, Cambridge, in June, 1640, was of this line.

Little John Mather, 1622

Richard Woodburn married the sister of John Mather, and when he died in 1622 he gave £10 to his nephew " little John Mather." Sixteen years later John Mather died. His will was spoken shortly before his life expired, to three persons, who repeated his wishes to the court in order to acquire for them legal force. Then it was said that " little John Mather " had not received his legacy and the father had directed that it was to be paid out of the whole of his goods. John Mather the father was a husbandman and weaver. In 1636 a kinsman, Hugh Mather, had died, poorly off. He had had a troublesome son, James, who had been very "chargeable" to him and in settlement of his filial portion the father left him 3s. 4d. When Hugh had disposed of his meagre stock of worldly goods, he wrote: And all things soe finished I have an assured hope to rest in joy unspeakable for ever and ever. Amen.—Posterity shares this his pious hope, too.

A Knighthood Fine, 1631

Charles I in the years preceding the Civil War raised taxes independently of Parliamentary consent, in an effort to establish absolutism. By distraint of knighthood a fine was imposed on those whose estates were adjudged of sufficient value to warrant the holder being dubbed knight. The Commission in Lancashire examined the value of certain Tyldesley lands and extracted a fine of £10 from John Tyldesley in September, 1631. This sum was a composition for having neglected to attend the coronation to have received the order of knighthood. John Tyldesley had leased out part of his ground to Thomas Risley sometime before 1617.

Francis Sherrington Buys Tyldesley Manor, 1634

The Andertons of Lostock held the Wardley part of Tyldesley Manor assigned to them by the agreement of 1572 to the year 1634. Christopher Anderton was then in possession as grandson of Christopher, the purchaser. On Monday in the fifth week of Lent, 1634, the grandson joined with Althea, his wife, and Hugh Macand in selling for £800 to Francis Sherrington the manor of Tyldesley, 10 messuages, 50 acres of land, 30 of meadow, 50 of pasture, 12 of wood, 40 of moor, 10 of moss, £3 rent of the tithes of grain and sheaves.

Garratt Corn Mill, 1635

The corn mill, which was a privilege of the manor of Garratt, is very old. It is first mentioned in 1301, when Hugh, son of Henry Tyldesley, was engaged in a case heard at York, on November 18, 1301, Henry agreeing to acknowledge Hugh's rights in the seven messuages, the mill, 86 acres of land, 10 of meadow, 160 of wood, and 26 of pasture, all in Tyldesley, which formed the subject matter of the claim.

Very much later in 1635 in the time of Robert Blundell, the corn mill figures again in a transfer. It was then particularised as a water mill, and in 1716 was let to Thomas Kay: it was still in use in 1838; John Babbington worked it as tenant of Lord Francis Egerton. There was an area of nearly three Cheshire acres assigned to it and a cottage with a room over the cottage. In addition to the waterpower of the brook there was a steam engine used as well to grind corn. Other millers were Abraham Grundy (1869), Renington (1871), and in 1872, Henry Richard Pennington. The gross rateable value of the mill was £90. Now it is derelict. When Chaddock assumed manorial dignity, there was a mill attached to this hall, but as no stream was adjacent, it had to be a windmill.

James Mann and His Welsh Cows, 1638

The Manns were tenants of the Tyldesleys of Wardley and were very numerous at one time in Tyldesley township. James Mann, or Monn, so known locally and so articulated, died in 1638; he left two sons, Christopher and William, two daughters, Ellen and Elizabeth, and a son base, Thomas. His wife's name was Elizabeth. His total wealth came to £71. 5s. 8d., but he had engaged himself under seal to pay to his wife's granddaughter, Ellen Leigh, in consideration of her marriage with Peter Rylands of Westhoughton, £5 worth of goods. When probate was obtained, the value of these goods was put at £32. 13s. 8d., which reduced the estate to only £38. 12s. James was styled husbandman; among his items were cutgroats and barleyflowers, 3s.; cheeses in Manchester, £1; silver spoons, a set of four, 19s.; and a lanthorn, 8d. His most valuable possession—three Welsh cows and a weaning calf at £10.

The Marshes of Shakerley, 1639

The Marsh family of Shakerley, distinct from their other kinsmen, lived in the subtownship for a long period. Ann Marsh was a widow who died in 1639; she had sons, Richard, Raph, and a son-in-law, Robert Makant. In 1663 this Richard Marsh died; he was a carpenter and his children, John, James, Peter, and Ellen. He asked Ellen to give 12d. each to the three children of his brother, Raph, and to the two daughters of Robert Makant. But John, the eldest, had to pay £10 each to his brothers and sister within three years after the father's death; if he did not, the others could enter on his farm for six years and recoup themselves for these sums; but they were to do all boons and services, pay all taxes and leys, keep that part of the "housing" in good repair and not to plough up the land. Richard was worth £68. 17s. 10d. In 1677 Oliver Marsh died; he was son of John and Frances; his widow was Margaret and his children, John, Raph, and Thomas. John, the eldest, was under age at his father's death. Raph, John, Margaret, and Anne were brothers and sisters of Oliver, who, when he died, left £62. 14s. 11d. Raph Marsh died in 1679, worth only a poor sum of £5. 19s. 4d. But it is Jennet Marsh of Shakerley, widow, who died in 1680, whose will is the most absorbing. She spoke of the " fire grate that standeth in my little house " and of " the coverlet of a mixed colour lying on my bed in the said little house and a Bible." Then among her legacies she gives to Mr. Thomas Crompton, Minister of Astley Chapel, 2s., which proves that Crompton, though ejected in 1662, had regained his living and was actually minister, when Jennet assented her will, March 4, 1679.

Tyldesley in 1641

On February 20, 1641, John Atherton convened all the men of Shakerley cum Tyldesley over the age of 18 in Leigh Church, there to administer to them the Oath of Protestation. The number who swore was 137, and their names reveal many of the old families. Nicholas Starkie of Cleworth Hall was the first to be sworn; later the two Chaddocks, Thomas and John, appear. There is no Shakerley in the list and only one Tyldesley, a Hugh. But there appear many of the time-honoured yeomen, the Makants, the Laylands, the Battersbys, the Parrs, the Manns, the Davenports, the Marshes, the Astleys, the Gillibrands, the Hursts, the Roscoes, the Smethursts, and the Sales, sturdy sons of those who from immemorial time had tilled the rich earth of the Banks, drenched with the history of their forbears.

Parr Brow, 1641

This slope of pastureland derived its name from the Parr family, who for successive generations dwelt here; their names figure in the Protestation and Association Oath Lists of 1641 and 1696.

Parr's Farm was a holding of 12 Cheshire acres in 1838 and belonged to William Speakman, with Mary Johnson as tenant. The same family gave its name to the bridge over the brook which marked the natural frontier of their estate, though sometimes the name Honksford is occasionally found. Joshua Hodgkinson died at Parr Fold on June 21, 1881. John Kay was at Parr Bridge Farm in 1881, and John H. Lilly in this century.

Arise ! Sir Thomas, 1643

The son of Elizabeth Tyldesley, widow and heretic, was Edward, born in 1585. He married Elizabeth Preston and entertained King James I at Myerscough Lodge in 1617. He died the next year. He was father of Thomas Tyldesley, the royalist. This great Tyldesley was a soldier, who learned his profession in Germany. When the Civil War broke out, Thomas threw in his lot with the King, Charles I. He fought at Edgehill and at Marston Moor. In 1643 he stormed Burton-on-Trent by crossing a bridge of 36 arches, while under constant fire. For this he was knighted, at Greenwich.

Cow Hire, 1646

A spinster in Shakerley, a neighbour of George Hurst, used to lend out cows. In this year she had hired out at least 13 beasts; she was Margaret Smith and when she died it was said that Margaret Mort was 8s. behind with her cowrent. All these cows out at pasture and milking were priced at various sums. This same spinster had four hives of bees, two standing in the garden of her brother, George, one out at Gyles Turtons, and the other at Thomas Farnworths. She left 20s. to Ellenbrook Chapel, 20s. to Mr. Harrop, preacher of God's word, and 6s. 8d. to vicar Gatley of Leigh, for her funeral sermon.

Geoffrey Shakerley, Royalist, 1646

Geoffrey Shakerley was another royalist who during the Civil War became one of the most ardent supporters of Charles I. For his opposition to Parliament he suffered sequestration of all his estates and was ordered to pay a fine of £1,960. He thought this too stiff and on March 13, 1647, he petitioned for a reduction. He declared in support of his request that after the surrender of Carnarvon he went home and took the National Covenant and the Negative Oath on August 20, 1646. As soon as he came of age he surrendered to Colonel Mitton before May, 1646, and now he asked the Committee for Lancashire and Cheshire not to sell his estates. He disclosed that besides his lands in Cheshire, there was the property in Shakerley and his rents there. In these his mother, Mrs. Margaret Shakerley had a life interest. There was the capital messuage of Shakerley Old Hall with the demesne lands, the corn mill, and the tithes of Shakerley and Tyldesley. These were worth before the war began £70 per annum. His old chief rents brought in £15. 7s. 2d., and the reversion of five nail smithies, annual value £2. 6s. 8d. He also drew 13s. 4d. out of Mr. Hilton's lands in Farnworth. The Committee men reduced the fine to £784. At the Restoration Geoffrey recovered his social balance. He became M.P. for the borough of Wigan in the Parliament of 1679 and was made Governor of Chester Castle. He died October 17, 1696.

A Petition Against the Earl and Sir Thomas, 1647

This petition was directed against the three great Lancashire royalists, James, Earl of Derby, the Lord Molyneux, and Sir Thomas Tyldesley. In its introduction it describes the Earl as the chief " incendiary " to civil war: it was signed by well-affected gentlemen and ministers in Lancashire. It made many accusations against them, of having acted most violently, burned many houses, shed much precious blood, and of having plundered and wasted the County daily. The petitioners were urging Parliament not to allow the Earl to compound. There were almost 600 signatures : on the dorse of each petition is the venue. The places were Hindley, Deane, Bolton, Denton, Radcliffe, Ringley, and Bury.

Thomas Higginson of Shakerley, University Fellow, 1648

The Shakerley family of Higginson were prosperous nailors. William was the grandfather of this scholar of Brasenose: " sick of body by reason of the Lord's favourable hand of correction imposed upon him " he died in 1596. His wife was Agnes and on the day before his marriage, he had agreed to a settlement of his property before the worshipful Geoffrey Shakerley, whom he asked to stand good and favourable according to that order and agreement and to keep it for the better upbringing of his children in virtue and religion. He appointed his wife and a Chowbent nailor Bonaventure Astley, " his beloved friend in Christ " to be executors. Thomas, his son, was industrious and when he died in 1638 he had lifted the family fortune from the £19 of his father to £243, a sum comparable with the estates of the Shakerleys, Chaddocks, and Garratt Tyldesleys. Thomas' wife was Elizabeth and there were four children, William, Thomas, Anne, and Joan. Thomas was sent to Cambridge, where on May 9, 1645, he was admitted a pensioner at Christ's. He later migrated to Brasenose, where he graduated B.A. in 1648 and the same year was elected Fellow. He became vicar of Church Minshull and was ejected in 1662. Only the very well-to-do in Tyldesley could afford a university training at this period for their sons.

A Stipend is Increased, 1649

The tithes of the parish of Leigh passed into lay ownership at the Dissolution and then that ownership eventually became subdivided between the local gentry. This plunder was in turn taken from them for their opposition to Parliament in the Civil War and diverted to other uses. One such use was to increase the stipends of ministers of the local chapels. On April 27, 1649, it was decided that James Smith, minister of Chowbent Chapel should receive an increase of £20 on his salary of £50. That increase came from the tithes, £8 of it from Leigh and £12 from those payable in Tyldesley and Shakerley.

The Death of Sir Thomas, 1651

The uncertain fortune of war brought Sir Thomas Tyldesley to the same fateful end as that of his royal master. After the execution of Charles I in 1649, Tyldesley was obliged to leave the country and he found shelter in Ireland and Scotland. When Prince Charles sought to stem the disasters of the unlucky House of Stuart, the Earl of Derby and Tyldesley crossed over and tried to win Lancashire for the royal cause. Parliament was too strong for them and the Earl's forces were outmanoeuvred in the narrow Wigan Lane on August 25, 1651, when Sir Thomas was slain. The Earl escaped through Wigan town. The body of Sir Thomas was brought to Leigh and buried in the Tyldesley Chantry of Leigh Parish Church. No note of the burial was ever made, but his family, after the Restoration raised a monument in his memory, which Bishop Pocock, an Irish bishop, saw in 1742. It was then sadly neglected. Cornet Rigby, who served under Sir Thomas built a monument in stone on the spot where his commander was killed, and the Tyldesley family kept this in repair for many years.

Lambert Tyldesley, 1652

Lambert was son of Thomas, who had died in 1638. His mother was a Starkie, and the young heir of Garratt was brought up at Huntroyde. He died unmarried in 1652, and his will was proved in London by his loving and kind grandfather, John Starkie, on December 1. He gave 20s. each to his uncles, John and Edmund Starkie, 3s. to every servant in the house at Huntroyde, £20 to his cousin, Susan Starkie, and to Robert Blundell of Ince Blundell 20s. The residue then went to the grandfather. Lambert's sister Elizabeth had died in 1650 and now Garratt Hall, its lands and services passed by descent to Marie, the younger sister of Thomas. She had married Thomas Stanley of Eccleston and the Stanleys henceforth continue the great line of Tyldesley as lords of Garratt.

Portrait of a Schoolmaster, 1653

Richard Worthington died in 1660: he was schoolmaster of Mort's school at Astley where he was teaching when he died. He was in Tyldesley as early as 1632, for on September 3 of that year he signed Henry Cowuppe's will. He lived in Henfold, next to his loving neighbour, William Partington. He was a careful man and had bought cottages in Astley and Sale. He had four children, John and George, Margaret and Dorothy; John had died before his father and had left three children, to whom the grandfather had assigned 13s. 4d. a year for their maintenance each until 21. At his death the feoffees of Morts School, " where I have for many years last past taught school " owed him £7. 0s. 6d. school rent. Many of his debts appear to be due from parents as fees. He died well-to-do, for his estate came to £90. 17s. 5d. Thomas Crompton, curate at Astley Chapel, was one of the witnesses of his will. He possessed many weapons, three guns, a caliver, a bill, a halberd, two swords, and two rapiers. An iron workloom figures among his properties. He had a pocket watch and a mural watch, a gold ring and a lodestone. He loved wine, and about the house was a sundial. His books were valued at £6. 4s. 6d. Across the dimness of centuries he appears to have lived well, to have been a militant roundhead, and a great humanitarian. He left £5 to the feoffees of Astley school to buy coal for the poor scholars there to warm them in the winter season and he charged the feoffees to build an outile annexed to the school within two years after his decease, otherwise the gift was to be void. His well-formed signature shows stolid character, worth, and sincerity.

Mary Stanley, Widow, of the Garratt, 1653

By 1653, Mary, the daughter of Lambert, was widowed. On May 23 in a plea of covenant she surrendered her rights in Garratt to Andrew Hall, Thomas Grey, and Richard Mascy, and received £40 in return. The extent of Garratt comprised at this date the hall, 12 messuages, two cottages, 10 tofts, 12 gardens, the water corn mill, 80 acres of land, 40 of meadow, 50 of pasture, 20 of wood, 38 of moss, and £8 in rents.

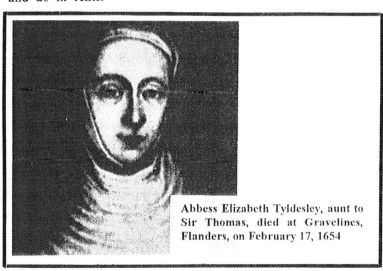

Abbess Elizabeth Tyldesley, aunt to Sir Thomas, died at Gravelines, Flanders, on February 17, 1654

Abbess Elizabeth Tyldesley, 1654

In the quaint diurnal of the English Claresses at Gravelines in Flanders are these two entries.

March 21, 1610. Item the same day and year made also her holy profession Sister Elizabeth Tyldesley, now called Sister Clare Mary Ann, being aged 24 years.

Much later, a different hand on a different page and on a sadder day wrote: In the year of our Lord, 1654, the 17 February in our afflicted Convent is happily deceased this Life Strengthened with the Rights of our Holy Mother Church Our Venerable and Most Dr Mother Abbess Sisr Clare Marie Ann in the 68th year of her age and 44 of her profession being one of the first that received the holly Habit in this Convent which she has governed in quality of Abbess the Space of 39 years very Laudably and peaceably and having ever given a very rare Example of all sorts of Vertues and Sanctity namely of an admirable prudence.

The Chained Fox, 1655

Edward Tyldesley, son of Sir Thomas, is said to have built a gabled house on the south shore at Blackpool about this year. It became the favourite residence of his son Thomas, who kept a fox chained at the door in lieu of a dog: hence arose the name of Fox Hall. This building, part of which still remains, has been converted into the Fox Hall Hotel and together with Tyldesley Road at Blackpool helps to keep alive the memory of these perished associations of a great past.

Arthur Parr, 1655

Arthur had as children, John, Samuel, Hester, and Mary. He died under the rule of the Protector Cromwell. He had acquired a close of ground, two acres, from Richard Dampford, a holding in socage tenure from a blacksmith of Tyldesley, Thomas Hodgkinson, and a lease of township land which had belonged to John Glover of Astley. At the date of the will in 1653 John, the eldest son was under age: to him went all the land on the death of his mother Elizabeth. Arthur had given certain milk beasts out at Thomas Laughs to John and Mary, but this bequest was discharged by the father, as they had already been given. The Parr family at this time surpassed all other families in Tyldesley in personal wealth.

Oliver Fold Farm, Boothstown, 1656

The old name for this farmstead was Oliversons; it formed part of the Chaddock lands and in 1656 Thomas Oliverson, husbandman, died here. He had three sons, Oliver, Thomas, and William, and a son Thomas Haddock in Ireland, who was left 10s. " in case he come over to the house and want the same." In 1595 Hugh Oliverson had lived at the farm. Thomas had goods worth £45. 8s. 3d.

King Charles II Grants a Pension to Lady Tyldesley, 1662

On December 18, 1662, Lady Frances, widow to Sir Thomas, asked the king for a pension. It was averred that her late husband was one of the first to rise up for King Charles I, losing thereby life and estate. He left her, the petitioner, destitute with nine small children. She asked for a pension of £300 for life. Lady Tyldesley's request was marked for reference to the Lord Treasurer, who advised one of £200. This was granted May 30, 1663.

The Laylands in Decline, 1665

The Layland family, who for centuries untold had lived on in virile strength as yeomen, declined in the latter half of the 17th century. Like the patrician families they were no longer able to prolong their vigorous stock. In 1663 Edmund Layland died; he left a widow, Elizabeth, and only £7. 4s. estate. He had no beasts, only a little barley and oats growing upon the ground. The most interesting item listed for probate were his butterprints, valued 2d. Two years later William Layland died; this William was a nailor, he left in all £32. 18s. 7d., of which £16. 15s. were debts due to him. John Layland, Thomas Marsh, Hugh Makant, and Thurstan Parr made the inventory, evidence which seems to show that the Laylands lived now in the eastern part of Tyldesley, where a small farm perpetuated their name to recent times.

Hurst Farm, Mosley Common, 1667

The Hurst family in this century begin to be located here in contrast to their namesakes in Shakerley. John Hurst died in 1667, and at that time Hurst Farm was divided. Ann, his widow, took the little house, the loft, and the chamber above it at the east end. John, the heir, had the great house from the wall and the stairs, which divided them. The widow took the old barn, the cowhouse, and the adjacent buildings, with the garden on the south side of the house, and the croft beside it. The son took the new barn, the old kitchen in the fold, the garden on the north side, and the croft to the east of it. Ann had in addition all the fields at the east end of the farm between the common and the brook, whether she married or not. John was left with the farther side of the common and all the damsides belonging to the fields. The fold was to be used in joint occupation and after Ann's death, the son took the whole. The estate came to the value of £43. 1s. 3d., and besides the usual husbandry and hustlement, there were worklooms, bees, a musket, and a musket barrel. Hugh Parr, Adam Grundy, and Adam Partington were witnesses of the will. This John Hurst occupied the farm to the year 1719, when he died. It was then stated that the house lay near to Mosley Common and extended to 10 acres. He possessed property of a value of £29. 13s. 7d.

Edward Tyldesley Writes to Samuel Pepys, 1667

Edward Tyldesley wrote on October 1 in this year to the great diarist, who was then Secretary of the Admiralty. He testified that Robert Withers and himself had surveyed Foudray Pill and a draft sketch was enclosed. Sir Thomas Strickland and Withers were to explain more fully the business in hand. The place was most suitable for building ships for the king's navy, and such timber was there as all England could not show.

Catholics in 1667

A view of all the convicted recusants in Leigh Parish was made in 1667, township by township. The lists for Tyldesley gave the following:

Lambert Bury.	Jane Sutton.
William Berry.	Katherine Hope, widow.
Elizabeth his wife.	Richard Hope.
Roger Hilton.	John Hope.
Elizabeth his wife.	Eleanor Partington.
Ann Hilton, widow.	James Holcroft.
Mary Hilton.	Emma, his wife.

Later, on June 2, 1679, the constables of Tyldesley, George Sidlow and Jeremiah Meanley, presented to the grand jury a smaller list of known recusants above the age of 14, who neither took the oath nor went to church, such were:

William Berry and Elizabeth, his wife.
Catherine Hope, widow, near 80 years of age.
John Hope, shoemaker.
John Holcroft, webster.

Shakerley Old Hall, in 1667

Shakerley Old Hall at this time was a magnificent home; its rooms given in the old records have the fragrance of a style both grand and gracious. There was the main room—the hall, then were added the brewhouse, cellar, parlour, buttery, cheese room, dairy, and larder. Over the great door was the gatehouse chamber and inside the quad the court chamber. Some of the rooms, like those of Worsley New Hall in the Victorian pride of the Ellesmeres, had colour names—the blue chamber and the green chamber. There was a dining room, closet, little storehouse, passage, stairhead chamber, best chamber, the mistress's chamber, and the maid's room, all given in faithful detail, each with the contents it displayed.

Guest Fold, 1670

The Guest family appear late in the history of Tyldesley township. About 1670 a John Guest was living at Shakerley, and from the tenancy of this farm fell ultimately the name. John Guest and Thomas swore the oath of 1646; then in 1742 Richard Guest paid poor rate of 3s. 3d. During this century the Guests abandoned their fold, for in 1838 Henry Barnes was tenant of the farm and its 15 Cheshire acres. Later William Ramsden built a commodious house near to the old site, but he took no lease from the owner. This house was affected by subsidence from working of the mines, and Ramsden left it to retire into Herefordshire, where he died. For a time Elias Dorning, mining agent of the Shakerley Collieries, lived at Guest Fold, and Peter Scholfied died there in 1845, aged 82. Daniel Morrison was the last occupier of the large house, which is now demolished.

The Shakerley Miller, 1671

Ellis Deane alias Astley was a migrant labourer. From May 1 to Michaelmas, 1670, he worked as a bricksetter in Cheshire; then he hired himself to Mrs. Gromsditch in the same county as a miller for his meat, drink, lodging, and wages £3 a year. Here he continued to April 28, 1671, when he came to Sir Geoffrey Shakerley's mill in Tyldesley. He married Joan Chamberlain from near Warrington and stayed in Shakerley to December, 1671, when he moved to a mill at Newton Heath near Manchester. The justices in session at Wigan ordered that Ellis was not settled in Tyldesley and the township was discharged from any liability to support him, should he fall on evil days.

The Tyldesley Regiment, 1671.

Sir Thomas Tyldesley raised regiments of his own, trainbands, and paid their charges, while on the service of the king. An echo of his regiment came in 1671, long after the day of his death. Richard Butler, a Lancashire man from Myerscough petitioned to be admitted to Charterhouse as a pensioner. He said that he had served in Sir Thomas' regiment; he was a prisoner of war for a long time; he had lost his estate worth £100 yearly, and when at the Restoration £60,000 was set aside for needy officers, his allotment was but £16.

John Battersby, of Shakerley, Minister of God's Word, 1671.

John Battersby was a scholar of Shakerley, who went to Oxford and who in 1671 graduated from Brasenose College. Battersby entered the church and in 1689 he is discovered as officiating at Adam Mort's chapel in Astley. He still lived on at his home in Shakerley, carrying out his pastoral work in Astley village. He died in the prime of life and was buried at Leigh on January 18, 1690.

Stirrup Brook Bridge, 1672.

About this time Stirrup Brook bridge was decayed, and the brook was so violent and deep that his majesty's subjects could not pass without danger to their lives and goods. The justices of the peace in session at Manchester ordered certain local persons to view the structure with workmen of skill and certify them what would be the cost of building a new one. The Ellenbrook flowed between the hundred of Salford and West Derby across the king's highway between the market towns of Leigh and Manchester. It was evidently not then known as Stirrup Brook Bridge.

King Edward's Coin, 1674

Adam Partington, a tailor, left £3 to the poor of Tyldesley and 10s. to the poor of Boothstown. He died in 1674 and wished to be buried in Eccles churchyard. He gave £30 and a 10s. piece of gold to John Hope of Booths, and a desk, box and looking-glass, and 20s. of King Edward coin to Margaret Morris of Heaton near Deane.

Adam had two apprentices, John Parkinson and William Cooke, and it was his desire that they should continue to be instructed by masters, who would teach them their mistery well; but the profit from their indentures was to go to his sister Elizabeth. His loving friends and neighbours, Thomas Arrowsmith and John Gillibrand were his appointed executors. At his death men owed him £16. 2s. 7d.; out at interest he had £15. 10s. John Hurst owed him £1. 17s. due at Christmas, and his ready money amounted to £3. 19s. Among his trade goods were four pairs of shears and a pressing iron value 4s., bands and cravats 1s. 6d., two brushes 1s., white nun's thread 2s., thread and jump buttons 1s., nine yards of buckram 1s. a yard, and 12 dozen of thread buttons 1s. The looking-glass of especial mention was priced 2s. 6d. and the desk 4s. His books came to £1. 2s.

Governess Tyldesley Arrives in Paris, 1675

The Diary of the English community of the Blue Nuns in Paris reveals this entry in 1675:

This year the two little Throckmorton with Miss Tillsly their governess came to be educated.

There were other members of the Tyldesley family in France at this time. Three of the daughters of Sir Thomas became nuns and Anne, one of them, rose to be lady abbess of the convent of the English Augustinians in Paris.

40

Highways, 1676

On October 26, 1676, the surveyors of Tyldesley made a report upon stretches of their roads, the usual and common highways. Leigh to Manchester, 165 roods; Chowbent to Manchester, 353 roods; Astley Chapel to Bolton, 203 roods and Leigh to Mosley Common 45 roods, all which lengths were narrow and less than 24 feet wide. In the following year, July 12, 1677, two justices certified the Ormskirk sessions that Coup Brow to Astley Road and Makants Lane were then sufficiently opened and repaired by the inhabitants of Tyldesley.

Garratt Hall Enfranchisements, 1677

A privilege enjoyed by Garratt as an ancient seat, manor house, and capital messuage was that its owner was exempt from being burdened with certain offices such as constable, overseer of the poor, and churchwarden. As lord of the manor he had more important duties of a public nature to perform. These inferior township offices were unpopular and in time objections were made against the exemption which Garratt enjoyed. ʼAn attack had been made in 1677, when the justices of the peace ordered that Thomas Stanley's estate should continue to be discharged from providing an overseer of the poor and that Thomas Marsh was to serve for that year. When the Stanleys leased Garratt to tenant farmers, there was less justification for the exemption. In 1689 Thomas Thropp was tenant of Richard Stanley: he successfully claimed his discharge in accordance with the old custom of the town, but this order was later set aside and Thropp had to act as overseer of the poor. In the margin of the petition it was noted that Mr. Chaddock had more interest in the commission than Mr. Stanley claimed, that the Starkies and other chartered tenants served and that New Hall, the more ancient estate, had been ordered to serve.

A Soap Maker, 1680

James Parr was a chapman, who from the evidence of his will specialised particularly in the manufacture of soap. He lived in the eastern part of Tyldesley, for Thomas Chaddock, Jnr., witnessed his will and added his signature. Of a total value of goods of £82, £40 of this represented soapash. He had at the date of his death 45lb. of tallow, 3d. per lb.; 29lb. of soft soap, 3d. per lb.; 33 dozen ball soap worth 13s., and 11 dozen of soap at 3d. per patten. Besides his soap he had quite a stock of tailoring materials. His reserve of candles, 31lb. was valued at 9s.

Industrial Injuries, 1681

Roger Dunster of Tyldesley, was a collier, who had the ill luck to be lamed in a coal pit and in consequence was under the doctor for over six months. He was poor, had a wife and two children. The overseers, to stave off his starvation were ordered to make him a reasonable allowance. Another miner, in 1707, James Smith, had been bruised by falling into a coal pit and there a basket of coals dropped upon him. He was as a result made weak and infirm. He had a wife and five children. To keep him and them alive, 8d. a week was granted till further variation.

James and Anne Astley, 1681

James Astley carried on the traditional family trade of a nailor, just as Thomas Astley, of Shakerley had done before 1579. James himself was buried at Leigh, May 12, 1681, and the next day his wife Anne was buried. This explains why in his goods there was this strange double item listed by his valuers: man's apparel, £1. 10s. and woman's apparel, £1. 10s. His goods came to £49. 5s. 9¾d.

Cleworth Hall, 1682

The Starkies, by the marriage of 1578, became possessed of Cleworth and during the next century it was one of their principal homes. Katherine, daughter of Lambert Tyldesley, who died in 1613, married Nicholas Starkie; he headed the oath list for Tyldesley in 1641. But towards the end of this century the Starkies left Tyldesley to reside more and more continuously at Huntroyde. For in 1682 Thomas Parkinson of Cleworth took his son Ralph for baptism at Leigh. Like Garratt and Shakerley Hall, Cleworth lost its prestige and became a farmhouse. Mrs. Higham was tenant in 1825 and Thomas Lowe in 1838. The Lowe family, still here in 1887, were followed by Richard Austin.

The Parr Family in the Days of Prosperity, 1684

The Parr family in the dying years of the 17th century, embarked on trade and came thereby to wealth. John Parr was a yeoman, who made his will in 1652 and died in 1663. Margaret Parr and his son John were executors. He left 5s. 8d. for a funeral sermon and 10s. to the poor of Tyldesley, where " most needful." His will is the second of the Parrs of Tyldesley which has kept ahead of the destruction of time. He was substantial by the standards of his day and left £235. 2s. 4d. In the shop at the farm there is no mention of any looms and the biggest feature of his estate were his leases and money set down at £86. 9s. As John died in the early year, his valuers faithfully inserted the expense of ploughing already done in the fields at £2. 5s. Hugh Parr, William Parr, and Hugh Makand were witnesses. Hugh Parr died in 1667; he possessed £88. 8s. 10d. of goods plus itemised debts of £113. 18s. 5d.; and he left all worklooms belonging to him in whose custody or keeping whatsoever to his son Thurstan. His inventory shows he had linen £4. 6s. 8d. and flax, £2. 14s., and his looms were put down at £3. In 1685 Samuel Parr died; he gave all his goods in Yorkshire, Manchester,

OLD CLEWORTH HALL, DESTROYED IN 1805

Wigan, and elsewhere to the three children of Matthew Lythgoe.
Parr's Farm then comprised a backhouse, a firehouse, kitchen,
buttery, room over the buttery, room over the house, parlour,
a chamber at the higher end of the house, parlour, shop, and
room over the shop. In the shop were the looms, which wove
the linen and cloth. Samuel had three pairs of looms, two wheels, a
swift, one pair of warping walls, two gigs, linen yarn on bobbins
worth £6. 10s. 4d., and linen yarn ready for weaving £49. 4s. 8d., and
cotton yarn £1. 7s. 1d. In the shop at Manchester and at the house
were goods value £26. 9s. 10d., and there were many large sums
representing stock in the hands of traders at Wigan, Chowbent,
and Manchester. His clock, musket, and lanthorn were assessed
together at £1. 3s. 10d. and his total estate came to £691. 1s. 1d. Thurstan, son of Hugh, died in 1695; he left a widow, Elizabeth, but no
children. His nieces and nephews were his legatees. He was engaged
in trade and had a pair of looms, but not on the same scale as
Samuel. His estate was worth £112. 17s. 6d.

Shoemakers, 1689

The Hopes were the shoemakers of Tyldesley in this century. William, the father, died in 1667 and his son, John, in 1689. Both carried on farming and husbandry besides their trade. There was a shop with an ark and seats in it and a value of leather of all sorts in 1667 of £3. 7s., and the leases and worktools came modestly to 5s. John, the son, possessed a pair of flails for winnowing. The estate of the father was £46 and that of his son, £65. The father's list of goods gives not only the value of his cows, but their names as well. Whitehead was worth £3, Cammill, £2. 13s. 4d., Valentine £2. 10s., Brandrock £1. 18s., and young Whitehead £1. 12s.

Francis Sherrington's Chief Rents in 1685

Francis Sherrington, who purchased a share of the manorial rights in Tyldesley, found that these in this year comprised several old chief rents. A list of these quit payments was made on August 10, 1685, and from it an idea of the decayed feudal pattern of Tyldesley is possible. The payments are:

Thos. Farnworth, 2s.	John Astley, 6d.
John Astley, 6d.	Starkey for Cleworth Hall, ½d.
Thos. Farnworth, 4d.	Richard Guest for Tho.
Geo. Sidlow, 3d.	Smethurst, 4d.
Henry Smith, 1s.	Thomas Sidlow, 4d.
Thos. Hamond, 1d.	John Marsh's widow for
Thos. Sidlow, 1d.	Henry Smith, 1s.
Arthur Parr, 3d.	Mr. Hamond for Sale House, 2d.
Thos Smethurst, 4d.	Widow Parr for Poor Meadow, 1d.
Hugh Makand, 2d.	Mr. Hamond for Stone House,
Robert Partington, 3s.	3s. 4d.
Mr. Mort of Damhouse, 1s.	Widow Makand, 2d.
Mr. Chaddock, 1s.	John Marsh, 2d.

Rights over Astley Manor, Chaddock, Cleworth, Smethursts, and Makants formed part of that lordship of Tyldesley Manor belonging to Wardley, a transfer brought about by the marriage in 1331 of Margaret Worsley and Thurstan Tyldesley. For Astley Manor held land within the boundary of Tyldesley. The poor meadow rent of 1d. was created as a result of Kathern Speakman. She was a widow of Bedford and by her will of October 3, 1679, she gave the income of £30 to the poor of Bedford and Tyldesley. Her trustees bought an enclosure from Francis Sherrington of 1¼ acres, the rent of which was to be given in relief of the poor. But on this field was held the reserved chief rent of 1d.

The list of payments on the left was comparative.

Stonehouse, 1685

This quaint homestead, still occupied, derives its name from the hand-trimmed stone of which it was built. A mullion window is a sign of its antiquity. In 1695 Thomas Hamond lived here and paid chief rent of 3s. 4d. to the lord of the manor. The same rent was paid by his successor in title, Henry Hampson in 1810 to the Bridgewater Trust. In 1838 Jeremiah Hampson was both owner and tenant. Its area then covered 15 Cheshire acres. Jeremiah died February 5, 1854, and John Hampson was drowned while drunk on November 8, 1857. In 1855 Jeremiah's brother-in-law, William Ratcliffe, tried to sell the place by auction at the Star and Garter; there was only one bid of £2,000, which was not taken. Ratcliffe lived at the house to December 18, 1856, when he left for Manchester; he returned two years later. Another tragedy occurred at Stonehouse on September 2, 1835, when James Hampson was drowned there. Elizabeth Hampson, who once resided at this farm, died October 29, 1870, aged 81. John Barlow was farmer in 1881, and Mrs. Elizabeth Barlow occurs in 1909.

Richard Bradshaw to the Poor of Tyldesley and Shakerley, 1685

Bradshaw, a benefactor of Leigh Free School, died in this year. Besides his bequests to that school and to the poor of Pennington, he gave by his will dated April 28, 1681, 20s. to the poor of Tyldesley and Shakerley, and a similar sum to the poor of Astley. His friend, Thomas Chaddock, witnessed the will.

Francis Sherrington Sells the Manor of Tyldesley, 1690

Sherrington on August 22, 1690, conveyed extensive properties to three purchasers, Alexander Radcliffe, and John and Peter Parr. Included in the sale was the manor of Tyldesley, one half of the manor of Westleigh and Pennington, and other property in Tyldesley and Westleigh. This part of the Tyldesley Manor eventually on March 18, 1722, came into the possession of George Kenyon, who paid £850 for it. The properties which passed by purchase embraced two messuages, 10 cottages, 10 gardens, 80 acres of land, 40 of meadow, 120 of pasture, 10 of wood, 10 of furze, and 200 of turbary, with the tithes of grain and sheaves, and 9s. 0½d. rent in Tyldesley, Booths, and Worsley. The Kenyons already possessed some property in this remote corner of the township. Lydia Wallwork, who died in 1667, held a cottage under Mr. Kenyon, which she assigned to her daughter Lydia for the residue at that time unexpired.

A list of old Tyldesley family signatures

Tho: Haddocke — 1680

Jeffery Shakerly — 1690

Ri worthington — 1653

Samuell Parr — 1684

William Hope — 1667

Henery Marsh — 1705

Samuel Mekand — 1706

Margaret Vernonn — 1664

George Ormerod — 1828

Thomas Hearsley — 1828

Peter Bent — 1840

James Rutter — 1833

Caleb Wright — 1888

Margaret Parr and the Minister of Chowbent Chapel, 1693

Margaret was widow of the rich Samuel; like him she died affluent and was worth £629. She was buried at Leigh, December 1, 1693, in defiance of her last wish to be interred at Bolton. She gave £5 to Matthew Lythgoe of Manchester. Her daughter, Mary, had married Jonathan Meanley; to her she left a twiggen chair, warming pan, silver spoon, side saddle and pillion, and all her linen and woollen apparel. Jonathan Meanley, her son-in-law, and Arthur Parr, her son, were her appointed executors. Among other bequests she gave 20s. to Mr. James Woods, Minister of Atherton Chapel, the father of the famous " General."

Henfold

The name Henfold has long been part of the local landscape; an early deed speaks of Hendam. The farmstead which gave its name to a locality existed in 1687 and was part of Garratt Hall estate. Joseph Calland was tenant in 1742 and in 1825 Peter Bromley. He was succeeded by Samuel Newton, who was a native of Ellenbrook and who attended the chapel there. He died October 19, 1846, aged 62, and his wife carried on for a time. James Unsworth was farmer in 1873 and early in this century James Grundy. The tithe map of 1847 shows much woodland round Henfold on the north, with a cottage standing on the site of the present Henfold House built by Walter Bridge. The farm disappeared in this century and the land was put to Tan pits. A small colliery was sunk by the Duke of Bridgewater in Henfold on the Astley boundary; it was working in 1838 and assessed at £217 for rates.

Local Hustings, April 18, 1693

It was agreed by the heads of the inhabitants of Tyldesley cum Shakerley, at their accustomed time and place where they usually meet for electing and choosing officers for the township, that by unanimous consent and mutual agreement Richard Marsh and Thurstan Parr should be overseers of the poor for 1693-4. The election was made on this day. John Gillibrand and John Mather, constables, William Partington, churchwarden, Jonathan Collier, overseer, and 15 others signed the note. Earlier, on November 1, 1682, Henry Marsh the elder of New Hall was elected constable for the lower side, and for the " harr " or higher side, Thomas Marsh and William Hindley. Seventeen townsmen were witness to the 1682 election and the old constables were duly discharged on that day. Overseers of the poor and constables were chosen by the inhabitants at different days of the year; but the surveyors of the

47

highways, after their turn of duty, could by custom nominate their successors. On May 1, 1682, Jeremiah Meanley chose George Smith to serve for Mrs. Starkie, widow. He claimed exemption as he was poor, farming Sutton ground, area six acres, which had had no house on it for a dozen years. He was discharged, and Meanley had to serve till the next quarter sessions. Service in these township offices was burdensome and troublesome. Nicholas Marsh and George Sidlow after their year of office in 1676–7, appointed John Hope and John Guest to follow on as surveyors of the highways. They refused: at the quarter sessions at Wigan they were bounden to take up the office on pain of a fine of £5 for refusing.

Mosley Common, 1695

This common once belonged to Tyldesley Manor; the name occurs very early and in 1301 it is given as Mosseld Yard or that area which had been cleared near to the Mosley brook. When Francis Sherrington sold the waste to his purchasers, Radcliffe and Parr, they agreed that no erection was to be made on the common. In 1696 Urian Cowper, a nailor, who was a native of Tyldesley, successfully petitioned the justices of the peace to allow him to build a cottage on the common and to make himself an enclosure as a defence against the rest of the waste, so as to form a fold or garden. The cheese charterer and the cheese lord and the freeholders of the township had given their consent. Urian built his cottage, and later in 1702, when the sayers assessed it for rates he appealed against a levy of 6d. As he was poor, it was ordered that he pay nothing. Then in 1713 Thomas Chaddock enclosed eight acres on the west end of the common. Radcliffe and Parr opposed him and the case went to arbitration. The award was that Chaddock could fence off and have the benefit of coal turves in his intake, but he had to pay Radcliffe and Parr a yearly rent of 1s. The area of Mosley Common in 1847 was 34 statute acres.

Moss O'Lee and Parr Bridges, 1696

The name for Moss O'Lee in 1696 was Hough Bridge. The highway supervisors had obtained from the justices of the peace by two payments £31. 9s. 8d. to rebuild it, and when all costs had been debited there remained a surplus of £1. 15s. 10½d., which was utilised for paving the ends of the bridge. Even this did not exhaust the sum and on October 10, 1699, a balance of 16s. 4½d. was paid into court. Matthew Hampson was the builder. On June 19, 1697, Richard Stanley of Garratt received 5s. for the land on which the bridge stood and Thomas Withington, his tenant at the hall, got 10s. 5d. for carting 17 loads of paving stones and sand. Included in the items were a new staff hedge, 2s., and 200 quickwood growths, 1s. Parr Bridge called Mosley Bridge at this period was also rebuilt in this year. The mason was Edward Heye and the stone came from Edgefold Delph, fully distant two-and-a-half miles. There had been allowed £20 for these works, but the estimate was exceeded by £6. 12s. 4d. and the two highway surveyors, John Gillibrand and Oliver Thomasson at Wigan, January 18, 1696, asked that they should be allowed this sum out of the moneys to be granted for the repair of any bridge within the hundred of West Derby in the near future.

Tyldesley in 1696

The men of Tyldesley cum Shakerley were in this year again convened in assembly to give oath and swear true loyalty to King William III. Sixty-five took the association oath, which on this occasion was administered by the township constables, William Partington and Giles Marsh. In Tyldesley there were no refusals. A scrutiny of the list shows only one inhabitant of the prominent old families—Thomas Chaddock. The rest, Tyldesleys, Shakerleys, Starkies, were gone and men of lesser stature were in the saddle. There were still the Davenports, Marshes, Manns, Hursts, Gillibrands, Astleys, Partingtons, Smethursts, Parrs, and Makants. Another generation or so and many of these were destined by the process of inevitable change to disappear for ever from that locality, where their forbears had laboured with sober moderation for so long.

William Mather, Innkeeper, 1696

Mather's Inn was in Shakerley. William had added a new house to his old one, which part he left to his son, Thomas. The widow, Margaret, was to live in the old part and after her death, Peter, a younger son, was to take possession. But Peter was forbidden to sell, let, or set his share, without first of all giving Thomas the right to bargain for it.

The Shakerley Miller, 1697

Henry Hindley, miller at Shakerley Mill, died in this year and was buried at Leigh, March 25. He left £53. 10s. George Astley was his landlord, under whom he had lived for many years. To George, son of his daughter Easter, he gave £5 towards binding him apprentice. The bulk of his property went to Hugh, who had been an obedient son and cared for his father both in sickness and health. Though Hindley was miller, his main wealth was in 89 ends of fustian cloth, valued at £38. Only his sieves, racks, and measures at the mill were particularised.

Nicholas Marsh and His Windows Tax, 1699

Nicholas Marsh of Turncroft petitioned on July 17 of this year for a reduction in his window duty. He claimed that his yeoman's house had only nine glass windows; he had been charged 6s. a year, whereas the proper tax was 2s.

The Makands had long been men of stund substance, out decay
set in on their ancient stock during the 17th century. Only one will
of the great number of Makants who appear in the unfolding pro-
cession of Tyldesley's local history has survived. This was made on
January 17, 1705, by Samuel Makand, yeoman. About a year later
he died. He left one half of his real estate to his mother, Mary, for
life. Sam was unmarried. He owed £32 to Nathan Mort of Chowbent, part of a purchase he had made, and he left his executors to
pay the debt out of the issues of his lands. Apart from the bequest to
his mother, he divided his property, one-third to his sister, Mary, and
two-thirds to his brother-in-law, John Hilton. He left 5s. to William
Marsh, son of John Marsh of Tyldesley, to buy himself a bible.
Edward Glover was another brother-in-law. This was his list of
goods: one pair of looms, 18s.; one light coloured colt, 16s.; one
brown colt, 10s.; one old colt, 4s.; a fustian frock, 3s. 4d.; one
pair of breeches, 5s.; one old paire of breeches, 6d.; stockens, 2s.;
one hatt, 1s.; one paire of shoone, 2s. 6d.; £3. 2s. 4d. Yet Sam,
unlike many richer testators, was able to write his name.

Ann Parr and the Apprentices of Astley, 1707

Ann, a spinster, was a farmer along with her brother John. She
died soon after her brother and a combined list of their properties
was given. There was a goodly sum of £174. 9s. due by bonds and
bills and the whole came to £257. 12s. 1d. Though Ann lived in
Tyldesley township she asked her executor, Oliver Hope, of Astley,
to invest £100 in land or rent charges, the yearly income to be used
for binding poor apprentices in Astley, and another £100, similarly
secured, the income to be paid to the overseer of Astley for the
benefit of the poor there. These bequests account for £200 of a
combined value of £257. And Ann, so charitably mindful of the
poor of a neighbouring township, cut all her " near relations,"
Elizabeth, wife of Richard Duckworth of Wigan, Thomas Parr,
Oliver Parr, Elizabeth Ashton, Henry Thomason, Thomas Leland
and his wife, and Thomas Ashton, each off with a shilling.

The Tanners of Tyldesley, 1710

From Ralph Mort, Tan Pits descended to Henry Mort, who died in
1710. Altogether for preparing hides and skins he had 10 pits, and
on January 12, 1710, this was the state of processing:

Pit	Hides				Tanning				Total		
	£	s.	d.		£	s.	d.		£	s.	d.
1 and 2	15	8	11	...	6	10	0	...	21	18	11
3	5	19	6	...	2	0	0	...	7	19	6
4	9	1	3	...	4	3	0	...	13	4	3
5	12	13	9	...	6	8	0	...	19	1	9
6	13	7	7	...	6	12	4	...	19	9	11
7	5	15	2	...	1	2	0	...	6	17	2
8	9	1	11	...	3	6	0	...	12	7	11
9	8	0	11	...	3	15	0	...	11	15	11
10	6	4	4	...	0	12	0	...	6	16	4

50

Robinson House, Shakerley, 1698

This house had been leased to the Marsh family by Sir Geoffrey Shakerley and in September, 1698, Ralph Marsh died there. He was a husbandman and moderately wealthy. He left to eight of the neediest poor of Tyldesley 20 yards of linen cloth to be distributed, for 10 years after his death on the feast of St. Martin, by his executors with the advice of the principal inhabitants and overseers of the poor. He shared Robinsons with his mother Frances, to whom he gave all his corn, whether in blade or grain, and all his hay. He assigned the lease to John Marsh of Bedford, only son of John Marsh. His brothers were John and Oliver and his sisters Ann and Margaret. The assignee of John Marsh died in 1699 and Robinson House then devolved on his son James, who had to pay Ann Marsh, his sister, £50 by five yearly sums, without claim to interest. As long as Ann stayed unmarried she had the right to live in the " little house " of Robinsons.

The King's Evil, 1702

The King's Evil was an affliction prevalent in olden times. In 1702 Margaret Dunster, daughter of a widowed mother of the same name, of Tyldesley, was sick of this distemper and bade fair to die, if she were not speedily relieved. She asked that the overseers of the poor be ordered to pay her 9d. a week assistance. The malady was said to be cured by a touch from the King, and was a form of tuberculosis.

Garratt Hall in 1702

Towards the close of the 17th century the Stanleys of Garratt forsook the patriarchal roof and went elsewhere to live. The hall and lands were let out for a term, and some years before 1702 Thomas Withington was farmer. At his death in this year his lease had still some time to run and he passed on the unexpired portion to his wife, Margaret, and his son, John. The rooms of Garratt were given as hall, parlour, little parlour, kitchen, buttery, and chamber above. The livestock on the farm embraced five horses, one colt, 24 cows, 22 heifers, four calves, 42 sheep, two pigs and a litter of five. In the kitchen were two looms. Withington was a trader on a large scale; he had bonds and bills worth £516 and £13. 7s. 1d. in book debts. The total estate was returned at £793. 7s. 1d., a substantial sum for his time and day. He had some desperate debts put down on December 28, 1702, at £8, and he gave portions as dowries to his daughters, Martha and Mary, of £100. His son William was under age at the date of his father's death. Withington was presented at Quarter Sessions at Wigan in October, 1689, by William Gillibrand, constable, for having bought an acre of standing corn. The charge was made, and Thomas Withington, badger, was given licence to buy growing corn upon the ground in contravention of the statute.

Besides this were green hides, dry hides, all tanned, value £38. 3s. 1d. The stacks of bark came to £60. Short hair and worklooms belonging to the tan house and mill came to £1. 10s. The total value of the personal property was £441. 8s. 10d., a good index to his wealth and standing. Tan pits descended to John Mort, and Ralph, a younger son, had the house and ground in Atherton. Eventually Ralph succeeded and when he died in 1746 the Tyldesley mill and pits were left to James Mort. Then the family went out and the business was carried on by Part and Monks. Baines describes the works in 1825 as being in Henfold foot, and William Sibberin was tanner. By 1838 he had been succeeded by Oliver Sibberin. The land assigned to the pits was seven Cheshire acres and the rateable value was £63. In 1860 Oliver discontinued the venture; he died August 31, 1861, aged 69, at Prospect House. Since that year the house and lands have been used as a farm. George Cheetham had the Tanyard Farm in 1873 and Hudsons appear in 1886.

The Three Crab Trees in Sale Lane, 1711

Sale Lane takes its name from a minor family; Ralph Sale, who was buried at Leigh in 1628, was a chapman, who had leased his plot of land for 99 years to Richard Thropp and John Kempe. Then in 1671 died Richard Sale: he was a blacksmith, and left only £10 13s. 4d. In 1711 George Sidlow lived in Sale Lane in a house with an acre of land attached. He was not rich and had been obliged to borrow £10 on mortgage for 500 years from John and Margaret Withington, of Astley. By trade he was a carpenter. To Alice, his wife, he left the east end of the house, the garden butt next to it, 20s. a year for 14 years, and the three crab trees in the hedge. But if Alice married again, she was to go off the " estete." All his worldly goods came to £4. 18s. 9d.

Oliver Thomasson to His Old Master, 1711

Oliver of Oliver Fold within Boothstown paid in this year his inevitable debt to mortality. He was of gentle piety and he gave 1d. to all the poor who came to his funeral and 2d. if they went to church to hear his funeral sermon. At his decease everyone was to have bread and drink at the house. To his nephew, Thomas Thomason, he bequeathed 5s. and his great bible; to Ann, his sister, the little bible, " and if she live a twelve month 5s. more." Oliver left a widow, Katheren, but no children. His nephew and niece were his chief legatees. Thomas Kay of the Garratt in Tyldesley and Mr. Thomas Chaddock were to be overseers of his will. To Kay and his old master, Thomas Chaddock, Oliver gave 10s. each " for their paines."

Owd Dog Lad, 1715

Edward Tyldesley's eldest son was called Thomas; he resided almost continuously in north Lancashire and had little to do with

Tyldesley and its neighbourhood. He was a great lover of the country and not very ambitious. His first wife was Eleanor Holcroft and by this marriage he became possessed of part of the Culcheth lands; his second was Mary Rigby, granddaughter of Cornet Rigby, who in gratitude erected the monument in Wigan Lane. This Thomas Tyldesley kept a diary and is known for differentiation as Thomas the diarist. His chief home was Myerscough Lodge, where in 1714 he built new stables, with the year and the inscription in stone—Old Dog Lad, the name by which he was known in the country. In Myerscough there was a massive fireplace with his initials " T. T." and the three coats of arms, the Tyldesley, Derby, and Manx. He was a slut-kisser of the mock corporation of Walton-le-Dale in 1708, and died in 1715. He is buried at Churchtown, near to Garstang.

A Carpenter of Boothstown, 1715

The Marsh family in the eastern part of Tyldesley, was settled at Turncroft, on the Chaddock estate and on the Garratt. This latter branch included Thomas, chapman, who died in 1688, possessed of a cottage held of Thomas Stanley of Great Eccleston for 99 years. He was well-off and left £278. At the date of his death one of his chests was at Garratt Hall. Elizabeth was his wife: she died in 1692 and her personal goods came to £133. 1s., their children were Thomas, William, Titus, Easter, Elizabeth, Anne, and Henry, who by 1692 was dead. Ellen, a granddaughter had been engaged in a lawsuit with Anne, her stepmother, and the grandmother had expended £3 in assisting her. This sum was duly deducted from her legacy of £4. 10s. Anne, the daughter, had married John Hope; Elizabeth, Thomas Chorton; and Easter, Thomas Farnworth. Besides these, there were grandchildren, Roger and Elizabeth Dickson, accounting for another unnamed daughter. Elizabeth's list of personal goods was a very large one, 162 entries and values in all and these give a fulsome picture of her goodly house in 1692, even down to a sword 1s. 6d., and bees at 6s. 8d. Later in 1715 Thomas Marsh died and his goods were valued by Isaac Marsh, John Hope, Joseph Parr, and John Guest. The total value was £77. 4s. 7d. Thomas was a dealer in timber and about the place were eight stores of timber. The first was in the field, the second near the gate, the third was all of ½in. boards, then one of spars, the sixth of beedends, the seventh of short timber, and the eighth of white wood boards. There were 40 yards of timber in the lane unbroken; 30 yards of pole in the garden; 30 yards of 1 in. boards at the shop, value 8d. per yard; five yards of ½in. at 3d. per yard; and another 24 yards at the shop of ½in. at the same price. He had 26 small planes, 3d. each; five large planes, 2s. each; a saw, 3s.; two benches and a lathe, locks, keys, and bands. At the time of his death, there was a press and a chest in the making and unfinished.

The Chaddock Marshes included Henry, who leased his tenement for 90 years; Isaac his son was to follow and then Katheren, the daughter, if it should hap they should live so long. Henry, a chapman, died in 1704: he lent Isaac £160 to buy Leyland's Farm. Isaac died before his father and left his brother Thomas as heir.

An Investment, 1716

In 1716 the chapelry of St. Helens received three benefactions, totalling £380, and with this sum the trustees entered the market to buy from the lay impropriators of tithes in Tyldesley sufficient to produce a yearly income of £30, to be paid to the curate as part of his stipend. In this round-off way did a part of the old church tithes find the same proper settlement for their enjoyment as intended for them in the very early beginnings of church history. Except this alien feature. The tithes of a parish grew payable by custom to the rector of the parish: here by repurchase they were paid until the year of commutation to a clerk who had nothing to do with either Leigh or Tyldesley township.

New Hall, 1716

New Hall, mentioned in William Partington's will of 1687, was in 1716 leased to Widow Heyes; it was then styled a mansion house. By 1742 this widow had left New Hall for Howcrofts and Thomas Smith was farmer in her place. He paid 5s. poor rate in that year. In 1838 John Lawton was tenant of Lord Francis Egerton; its acreage was 23 Cheshire acres. In 1853 Richard Grundy began his long association with New Hall; from him came the local name of "Dicky Beefs," a name by which the older generation still remember it, with affection. Richard died in March, 1872, and was buried at St. George's. In 1909 John Lomax was farmer here.

Anne Stanley's Annuity, 1717

Anne in 1717 was the widow of Richard Stanley, the heir of the ponderous traditions of the Tyldesleys. She was living at this time in Culcheth, and as she was Catholic she had to register with the authorities her income and her property. She stated in her return that she had an annuity for life of £118. 15s. payable out of Garratt Hall estate and its lands.

Abraham Collier, Overseer of the Poor, 1725

Abraham in 1725 acted as overseer of the poor for Tyldesley township. It was his duty to receive from the poor rate levy enough that would meet his expenses for the year, and no more. The accounts have survived for his year and these give a detailed picture of how poor relief was distributed in his day. He spent altogether £40 10s. 10½d. and his expenses covered the burial of paupers, paying

NEW HALL, TYLDESLEY. THE PROPERTY OF
THOMAS TYLDESLEY. SERGEANT-AT-LAW
TO KING HENRY IV, 1410

rent in time of sickness, buying medicine, making weekly payments
in illness, arranging home help for the aged, and the apprenticing
of poor children before magistrates. Abraham's receipts, when
written up, were in anything but chronological order and the cost of
enditing them was 1s. During his overseership he went to see Squire
Shakerley on some business and spent 5s. At another time he met
the Worsley men at the old chapel of Ellenbrook and spent 3s. 6d.
On May 1 he " flitted " Ellen Stirrup at a cost of 1s. Miles Barrett,
William Gillibrand, and Richard Guest checked his accounts.
Abraham was a yeoman, he died in 1745, and administration of his
goods was given to his widow, Amy, who could not write. John
Aldred and Thomas Marsh entered into a bond of £200 ensuring
the true disposal of the estate.

Parr's Charity, 1726

John Parr left 40s. a year to be paid to poor persons living in Tyldesley and Hurst. The indenture perpetuating the charge was dated March 2, 1729. Thomas Arrowsmith and Thomas Marsh were first trustees, to whom were conveyed the fields known as Bareley, the Meadow, Kiln Field, Three Rood, Hemp Croft, and the Ryding, containing 12 acres, but 40s. was to be paid each February 2 out of the Ryding to the trustees for distribution. When the Commissioners made their enquiry in 1828 William Speakman had been owner of these fields for some time and he had made the payments to the poor. But for five–six years prior to their visit, William Johnson the tenant of the land had given it away in accordance with the terms of the bequest. The fields form part of Parr's Farm, which Speakman had bought some " 20–30 years " before 1828. Ten years later both Speakman and Johnson were dead and Mary Johnson was in occupation.

The Stonemason at the Delph, 1727

The old surname of Cowoppe suffered many transmutations: it changed to Cowper and Cooper and later to Coupe—its modern topographical name. The Coopers were proud of their little farmstead which they described as " this good absolute and indefeasable estate of inheritance." In 1727 Urian Cooper had died; he was described as yeoman. He had five acres of land and a cottage in the possession of Richard Smethurst. His son, Urian, was under age at the time of his father's death and in his upbringing he was to be kept strictly to school and church according to the usage of the Church of England and not otherwise. Joshua Cooper had a son Urian, to whom the farm was left in default of a direct successor. In the same year of 1727, Joseph Cooper died; he was both blacksmith and stonemason. He possessed an anvil, rod iron, bellow tow iron, and lead in his shop. But from his list of materials it is clear that he was quarrying in the Delph. Here at the time of his death his most valuable item was 20 yards of hewn stone for a bridge in Worsley, valued at £2. Besides these, he had ashlar flags, 13 yards of gutter stone, eight yards of rattling, four pairs of cod stones, nine stone steps, one corner stone, two cheese press stones, two gate stoods, three broad flags, rubbish stones, a cheese press bottom, and a crane rope.

56

Thomas Johnson Buys the Banks, 1728

Thomas Johnson hailed from Bolton. In 1728 he bought " Bongs " and in 1742 he added to his estate by acquisition of land from the representatives of the Stanleys of Garratt. In 1752 he purchased Davenports. Thomas' son and heir died in 1763 and Thomas, the father, in 1764; the heir was a grandson also named Thomas. He died without issue in 1823. His property was inherited by his sister, Elizabeth, who had married George Ormerod of Bury. The " Bongs " estate lay on both sides of Elliott Street, as far as Shuttle Street, where it marched with the Shakerley estates.

Grace Chaddock, 1731

The long line of the house of Chaddock came to an end in 1723. Like many families of established and ancient descent the pedigree closed with a lass. Thomas Chaddock is mentioned in 1443, then in 1526 John and Hugh sold off an estate to the executors of Sir Thomas Butler. Adam Chaddock was churchwarden at Leigh in 1601, and Thomas was buried there in 1607. In the 1641 list are John and Thomas; this latter entered his arms at the Herald's visitation in 1664 and took his sons, William, Joseph, and Benjamin to be baptised at Leigh in 1674, 1677, and 1680. The spelling in these entries marks the end of the old pronunciation of Chaydock, and Chaddock henceforth becomes general. Thomas had a servant, Daniel Askew, who was involved in affiliation proceedings with Margery Aldred in 1677. He was unable to obtain any sureties for his appearance at Wigan sessions and was sent to gaol at Lancaster. While here he asked for his clothes to be forwarded on, and also 20s. wages, which his master owed to him. It was said that he was likely to perish for want of food.

Other families sometimes lived at the Hall. Geoffrey Holcroft was buried at Leigh from there in 1665, and in 1683 Thomas Haughton was living there. Roger Lowe the diarist mentions John Chaddock who was lying ill at Mr. Whitehead's in Astley on April 12, 1663. Thomas Chaddock took the oath in 1696. He was the encroacher on Mosley Common. He sent his namesake son to Brasenose College, where he became B.A., and in 1692 was instituted vicar of Eccles. This Thomas died in 1723 and left an only daughter, Grace. She married Miles Barrett, curate of Astley Chapel. On October 1, 1728, she mortgaged Chaddock, its lands, and two messuages to Joseph Byrom of Manchester. Grace married for her second husband Jacob Markland, and on September 25, 1731, they sold Chaddock Hall, its windmill, and the two farms of Thomasons and Olivers to Samuel Clowes of Manchester, for £700.

The Last of the Tyldesleys of Garratt, 1732

Thomas Stanley was the last of the long line of Tyldesley of Garratt. He was Catholic and Jacobite; he took part in the 1715 rebellion, which sought to restore the Old Pretender to the throne. After the rising was crushed he was attainted of treason and declared an outlaw. He maintained a precarious hold upon his lands, but progressive poverty, accentuated by penal legislation, forced him in 1732 to sell Garratt Hall to Thomas Clowes, a merchant of Manchester. The price paid for Garratt was £4,585. In this sad way did the last of the long great line of Tyldesley of Tyldesley Manor, Nicholas Manor, Garratt, Wardley, and Morley lose that grand inheritance of such enviable distinction and step down to mingle with the common herd.

Edward Tyldesley's Estate, 1736

Edward, old dog lad's eldest son, died in 1736. He had married Dorothy and was succeeded by his son, James. In 1717 the estate of Edward had been returned as of a yearly value of £720. 9s. 2d., and was said to issue out of the leasehold estate of Myerscough Lodge and out of a moiety of the manor of Holcroft in fee.

Yew Tree Farm, 1742

Yew Tree stood in the original Sale Lane; in 1742 John Meadowcroft paid 6s. poor rate. By 1838 Ratcliffe was the owner, and the farmer, David Grundy. Grundy was killed by his own cart, November 4, 1848. The extent of the holding was about 18 Cheshire acres. It was here in 1845 that George Green, of Wharton Hall, took a trial lease, prospected for coal and sunk a shaft. From his endeavours sprang into being the Yew Tree Colliery, and the later pits which operated under the name of the Tyldesley Coal Co. Ltd. The 1847 map shows much woodland along the road frontage. Charlotte Grundy was at Yew Tree in 1858, and Richard Hurst in 1881. With the encroachments of the colliery the farmstead disappeared.

Nuttalls, 1742

This modest home in Squire's Lane paid 2s. rates in 1742. James Nuttall was then the occupant. By 1838 Thomas Kearsley, the cotton spinner had acquired it. The area was about one acre and William Grundy was tenant. He was followed by James Hilton, who occurs in 1847, and later James Elliott made the little holding into a market garden.

Crow Bank, 1742

Crow Bank in Shakerley is mentioned in 1742 when it paid 4½d. poor relief. No occupant was then named. In 1838 Joseph Harrison was tenant of the Fletchers, the area extended to 25 statute acres and the rateable value was £44. Richard Harrison died here January 23, 1841. The barrel of a gun burst on October 16, 1848, at Crow Bank and killed John Watson, who had followed on as tenant. Then later came Thomas and Henry Kniveton, who besides farming, sold explosives and gunpowder from their magazine in the fields to the local colliery proprietors.

Common Fold, 1742

For the convenience of the tenants of Shakerley Hall two commons were set aside, one serving a ring of farms to the north-east of the hall, and the other much smaller lay to the south and was known as Little Shakerley Common. Common Fold derived its name from the nearness of the greater common. The farmstead in 1742 was tenanted by James Marsh. By the year 1838 the land had been split up and Daniel Hindley tilled four Cheshire acres, while the remaining 16 were taken over by Thomas Kearsley, who underlet the house to James Lee. Races were run on Shakerley Common to the year 1788. Later, the commons land was enclosed and appropriated to private ownership. Jonathan Hindley was tenant in 1881, Waddingtons in 1886, and Stevensons in 1888.

Tyldesley in 1742

James Marsh and Richard Guest were the collectors of the poor rate in Tyldesley for 1742. The township was divided into the higher side and the lower side. From the higher they took £5. 19s. 10½d. and from the lower £6. 3s. The two highest rated houses in the township at this time were Shakerley Hall, 19s. 3d., and Garratt Hall, 18s. 6d.

Shakerley Old Hall, 1742

Shorn of its ancient dignity, the hall became a farmhouse with a succession of tenant farmers. Of these there is mention in 1742 of Richard Jolley, in 1825 John Crompton, and in 1838 Thomas Kearsley rented the house and fields from the Fletchers. Isaac Grundy appears in 1847, and in 1881 Alfred Grundy. At the close of the century the same family was still here.

A Yeoman of Garratt Hall, 1748

During the years of the 18th century the great manor house of Garratt declined and became a farm tenanted by yeomen. One of the earliest of these tenants was John Edge. He was in tenantal occupation in 1742 and he died in 1748. He gave £10 a year to his widow, but if she remarried, only £6. To his daughters, Mary and Betty, he assigned portions of £210. To Ellen Hope, another daughter, likewise £210, but the executors were not to give £100 of this, in lieu they had to pay £5 a year, provided the father-in-law gave a similar sum until the whole was discharged. The widow, Ann, was to have one bed and bedstocks and enough furniture for one room. Edge possessed a house on lease in Shakerley and also the freehold of Berrys; if this came to be sold Thomas Clough was to have the first option to refuse.

Arthur Parr and the Local Ministers, 1749

Arthur Parr of Tyldesley died in 1749 and judged by the standards of his day he was well-to-do. Out of his many bequests he left individual legacies of £5 each to five local ministers. These were the preachers of his choice—Sedgwick of Chowbent Chapel, Valentine at Wharton Chapel, Mawdesley at Astley Chapel, vicar Farrington of Leigh, and Richard Meanley at One of Witches. To James Leigh, a clockmaker, he devised a like sum, and as a dole to each of the townships in Leigh parish 15s. each, but to Tyldesley with Shakerley 30s.

John Wesley Makes a Convert in Shakerley, June 15, 1752

Wesley, in his tireless peregrinations came to Shakerley four times. The first occasion was on Sunday, May 28, 1748, when after being stoned at the Cross in Bolton, he rode on to Shakerley. The subtownship was at this time the most populous and the most industrialised district within Tyldesley. He arrived before 5 p.m. and before 6 p.m. an abundance of people had gathered to hear him. He came again Thursday, October 19, 1749, again from Bolton, where he had preached under the open sky in a meadow. He spoke at Shakerley and then went on to Davyhulme. His third visit was on Wednesday, April 10, 1751; the last time he came was on Monday, June 15, 1752. It was about noon when he preached on that day at an old man's house near Shakerley. This convert was groaning for redemption and after the sermon he walked with Wesley a little way. From the hour of parting " the power of God fell upon him, so that he hardly knew whether he was on earth or in heaven—and from that time he was continually filled with peace and joy in believing." In this way did protestant dissent graft itself on Shakerley; a band of brotherhood was formed and the first certification of a house authorised for their meetings in Shakerley occurs in 1770.

The Protestant Dissenters, 1770

Shakerley had always been a hotbed of dissent and Wesleyanism throve there long before there was any separate buildings where worshippers of the same mind and conscience could come together. A house was officially certified to the authorities as being licensed for the meetings of protestant dissenters. It was notified on December 27, by Mark Scholfield; its location was somewhere in Shakerley.

Greenfield, 1771

Greenfield, geographically allied more to Atherton than to Shakerley, was in this year leased at a rent of £18 to Peter Marsh. Its area was almost 10 Cheshire acres. Peter Shakerley was the owner, and the 21 years lease expiring in 1792 was renewed by Charles Watkin and John Shakerley. There was a cottage attached to the farm, where Betty Marsh lived in 1838. Successive Peters of the Marsh family lived at Greenfield and as late as 1873 Peter Marsh was farmer here. Samuel Marsh, who strove so hard to re-establish his family's title to Turncroft, died at Greenfield in 1887 at the age of 63. His younger brother Peter, patriarch of a large family, was the father of John Marsh who died in 1947. From Peter the lease passed to his youngest brother Lawrence. His daughter, Florence, married James Blears, who was at Greenfield in 1902.

Samuel Clowes, 1773

Clowes was a merchant of Manchester; he bought up much real estate in Tyldesley during the 18th century. In 1721 he purchased Booths Hall from Helen and John Radcliffe, together with the manor of Tyldesley and certain old rents. In 1731 he bought Chaddock, and in 1731 Thomas Clowes acquired Garratt. At the rebuilding of Astley Chapel in 1760 Samuel and Thomas Clowes had two full sized pews assigned to them and two ordinary for the use of their servants. The Clowes let Chaddock and in 1742 John Hope paid 6s. poor rate. Samuel Clowes died August 5, 1773, the day appointed for the signing of his will. He was then living at Smedley in Yorkshire and he bequeathed the estates of Booths, Chaddock, with two seats in Astley Chapel and one in Leigh Church and Westleigh Hall to his grandson Samuel. In 1810 Chaddock was sold by auction at the house of William Davenport at Stirrup Brook. It was acquired by Richard Haldane Bradshaw and became later part of the Ellesmere estates. John Hope died at Chaddock in 1798, and in 1825 a cotton manufacturer, J. Smith, was living there. In 1838 Robert Smith of the Delph Mill was tenant of Lord Francis Egerton. Later came Mrs. Gretton, who in 1869 paid £100 rent. The hall was to let again in 1877 for £112 per year. Hurst at Yew Tree Farm had the land, for which he paid £36 a year, and there were two cottages included in the major tenancy. The Rev. Richard Hopwood in 1881, R. L. Harrison in 1885, John Orme in 1890, Harold G. Murray in 1909, and Benjamin D. Blakemore in 1924 were some of the later tenants.

Great Boys, 1778

Great Boys by its name perpetuates a bygone Norman influence. The estate is mentioned in 1778 and is detailed as " a messuage with eight Cheshire acres of land situate in Tyldesley-cum-Shakerley in the Parish of Leigh called Grate Boys, the dwellinghouse consists of three bays and the outhouses lying contiguous of five bays, there is a garden and orchard in one piece of ground lying to the south and west of the house. This estate is bounded on the east by an highway called Makins Lane, on the west by Cleworth Hall estate, on the north by Bank House estate and on the south by Morts and Sidlows estates." The old Roman road runs across Great Boys field. In 1838 the farmhouse had disappeared and James Dunster of Astley had the occupancy of the land. Soon after, a small colliery was sunk in the north-east corner of the estate. The farm formed part of the endowment of Astley Chapel. The colliery existed in 1848 and was begun by the Fletchers, who acquired the Shakerley property in 1836. It exhausted only the near-surface seams; the deeper mines were taken by the firm of James Roscoe and Sons of New Lester Colliery. Fletchers were working the Great Boys in 1877, when an explosion in that year cost seven men their lives. Harriet Berry was tenant of the farm in 1902 and Joseph Berry in 1909.

The Cost of a Pew in Astley Chapel, 1778

Many townsmen of Tyldesley resorted to Astley for public worship in the days before the building of the Huntingdon chapel in the square. Thomas Guest, a farmer of Tyldesley, had the exclusive right to a pew in Astley Chapel. The 1760 consecration plan shows a Thomas Guest pew on the south side as well as one in the gallery. Whichever it was, Thomas the farmer, left it to his son Abram, but the son had to pay the grandson Abram £2. 15s. for it.

The Flaming Castle, 1778

The Castle Inn in Tyldesley dates from this year. Jonathan Atkin built it and in 1825 Rosa Atkin was living here. She was found dead in bed, January 7, 1845. There was a bowling green in front of the inn, which in 1825 was taken away to form the church-yard of the church of St. George. In 1845 John Aldred was tenant: he died soon after and Betsy Aldred was at the inn in 1847. In 1853 Richard Crank is named. Later came Henry Andrew in 1858 and he was followed by Ann Andrew. John Hope appears in 1879 and Jane Hope in 1890. In this year the hotel was auctioned and sold to Mr. Bullough for £3,450. John Henry Makin was landlord of the Castle in the early years of this century.

George and Dragon, 1781

The George and Dragon is an old inn in Tyldesley. In 1781 David Atkin leased a plot of land at a rent of 13s. from Thomas

Johnson and built his dwellinghouses, brewhouse, and public rooms. Not having enough money he borrowed £80 from William Eckersley. The devisees of Atkin sold the inn for £161 to James Aldred, and five years later he sold it back to Francis Atkin, a personal representative of David. Francis Atkin lived at the " Green Dragon," for like other inns it changed its name, from 1795-1841. He mortgaged it in 1827 for £100 to Samuel Newton of Atherton, and this sum was still owing when the inn was put up for auction in 1852. Ottiwell Harrison was then publican; as he was executor of the will of Atkin he joined with Joseph Atkin of Liverpool and the executor of Newton in a sale for £640 to Thomas Morris, a brewer of Wigan. This brewery known as Henry Robinson and Co. was acquired by the Bolton firm of Magee Marshall and Co. Ltd., the present owners of the hotel. The old inn was taken down and set back in 1904 and completely rebuilt at a cost of £6,500.

Warrington School Land Lease, 1782

A lease of the date, December 25, 1782, was made by the Rev. Edward Owen, M.A., Master of the Boteler School, and five of his trustees on the one part and Samuel Clowes, of Chaddock, on the other part. The lease was of Grundy's Farm, area 15 acres, and Urmston's Farm, area eight acres, the term 99 years, or for the lives of Samuel Clowes, aged seven, John Clowes, aged five, and William Legh Clowes aged three; if any of them should so long live, timber and mines excepted. The rent payable was £14. 14s. per annum. The minerals had already been leased to the Duke of Bridgewater, who had engaged himself to pay a minimum rent of £50 each year.

Shakerley Corn Mill, 1785

Shakerley Manor shook off its feudal dependence on the manor of Tyldesley, whereby it was obliged to send all the corn grown in Shakerley hamlet to be ground at the manor mill. The possession of a water corn mill helped Shakerley Old Hall to become a reputed manor. The mill finds a mention in 1656, but it was existent much earlier. On December 11, 1785, a lease of the old mill was made by the executor of James Hart to Joseph Adkin and the yearly rent paid was £16. 16s. In 1811 John Ratcliffe was tenant; the building ceased by then to be used as a corn mill and had been converted into a carding and spinning shed. After this date, the old mill was made into cottages, which were standing until quite recent times. The Tyrers and Hampsons lived for many years in these old structures.

Fulwell House, 1792

It was about this date that Mr. Gregory erected Fulwell House opposite to Davenports in the west end. Gregory was a manufacturer. In 1825 Thomas Kearsley was the owner. He entertained here the Bishop of Chester when he came to consecrate the church

FULWELL HOUSE. THE HOME OF THE GREAT
INDUSTRIAL MAGNATES. DEMOLISHED 1935

of St. George. The house was a substantial one, 2½ acres in area, and described as consisting of kitchen, washhouse, mangle, coach and saddle houses, stables, shippons, and hay shed with a gross value for rates of £82. Kearsley was followed at Fulwell by John Jackson, of the firm of Jackson, Bayley, and Knott. Then came James Bayley, who died at the house on April 9, 1862. His widow Ann continued the residence. By 1871 this house of the great cotton magnates had been acquired by Charles Eckersley, who died in 1920. Two years later his son, William, offered the Fulwell and its grounds to Tyldesley Council, but the gift was refused by the narrowest of majorities. After a period of no occupation, George Clapperton became tenant and in 1935 the house was demolished. The vicar of Tyldesley, George Richards, was occupant of Fulwell in 1854: the churchwardens had agreed to make him a grant of £25 a year towards the rent.

The Lady Huntingdon Chapel, 1798

In the 18th century, that great age of dissent, Lady Selina Huntingdon shaped great ambitions; she had been much influenced by Wesleyanism, and she set about the establishment of chapels in different parts of the land, distinct in dogma and teaching from either Wesley or the national church, and began to arrange for their endowments and ministration. In 1783 six ardent young preachers were ordained at Spa Fields Chapel, London, and of these, J. Johnson, Tyldesley chapel's first minister was one. Somehow Thomas Johnson began to be interested and he proved a practical helper. He gave a site area of 1,300 square yards of land and all the bricks and sand necessary for the structure, plus a monetary gift of £200. Minister Johnson had a very eventful career. The building of a chapel meant a command over funds, which he imagined could easily be created; like others before him, he pledged his credit too freely and it is said he languished as a martyr to the new cause in Lancaster gaol because of the mountain of debt incurred by this new chapel in Tyldesley, Lancashire. Johnson was minister from 1789 to 1798, when he left to go to Manchester, where he died. He built a strange looking house for himself in the fields at the bottom of Astley Street, which long went by the name of " Bottom Chapel " in contrast to " Top Chapel " on the rise of the Banks. The whole style of this domicile was of a clerical flavour. At first, the worshippers of Tyldesley Chapel called themselves episcopal seceders; by 1825, when David Atkin was minister they were known as Calvinists. How long the ministers climbed up and down the hill to their chapel at the top is not disclosed, but Minister John Langridge lived in Lime Street in 1838 and paid rent to Thomas Fray. A very prolix trust deed was drawn up on May 31, 1798; this was renewed in 1857 upon the appointment of new trustees to bring up the number to 12. Of these early true stalwarts, two names became famous—John Grundy and George Green. At some later date a house in Johnson Street was purchased for the dignity and occupation of the chapel minister. The trustees were empowered to select their own parson and on Whit-Sunday he was to preach a charity sermon for the general support of the Sunday School. Thomas Johnson of the Banks put in the south gallery, the organ was installed in 1861, next year the north and east galleries were built, and last of all, in 1887, the west one. Crook, who was minister from 1880-9 made many structural alterations. The township constables set up the punishment stocks outside the chapel in 1784; these were removed in 1834, when the palisades were erected. In 1894 G. T. B. Ormerod enlarged the gift of the original site by donating a narrow strip of land to the rear.

BOTTOM CHAPEL. THE HOUSE OF MINISTER JOHNSON.
NOW DEMOLISHED.

The Governor of the Workhouse, 1798

Mark Scholfield was governor of the workhouse for Tyldesley from at least this year to at least 1809. Before the setting up of Leigh Union in 1837 each township had its own house for the poor. This place was rightly styled " workhouse " because the inmates, unless incapacitated had to work both outside and inside and the profit from their labour diminished the costs of maintenance. The house had its looms where weaving was done, and on July 24, 1798, Ralph Smith earned 6s. 6d. for his weaving and on the 13 August, the same name, but junior, 3s. Ralph, evidently the father, was sent on August 18 to James Nuttall, who paid to the governor 5s. for five days' work clipping sheep. The biggest revenue of the house came from the factories, especially from Peter Eckersley and James Arrowsmith, local manufacturers. On the contra side are the out-goings—coal, milk, meal, liquor, necessaries, making and repairing of shoes, candles, soap, starch, gift money to children and inmates who worked, snuff, tobacco, clothes, manure, potatoes, onion, cabbage, and carrot seeds. On October 7, 1802, a pig was bought for £3. 6s. 7d. and a tub of butter at £1. 5s. on November 4. The governor's salary rose from £1 per month in 1798 to £1. 18s. in May, 1808. Sometimes he had to pay the fines of paupers, who broke the sabbath. Samuel Harrison's fine of 1s. was entered up on May 6, 1802. Jonathan Hilton's club money £1 was paid out of the poor rate July 25, 1802, and James Partington got £1. 3s. to make up his arrears. The matron was Alice Heyes. Her wage was 8s. a month in 1800, and on one occasion she requisitioned for a watch, cost 5s., which was bought for her. In 1840 the average cost of maintenance per pauper in Leigh Union was 2s. 0½d. per week. Tyldesley house was calling on the rate for all this period, 1798-1809, except on two occasions in 1801 and one in 1805. Early in 1809 there was a slight credit balance of 4s. 8d. May 5, 1808, was purchased a pig for £1. 10s. and 147lb. of bacon at 7d.per lb. Jonathan Gerrard supplied milk to the house in 1801, when Richard Ormerod began to have the contract. Sometimes outdoor relief was given, and Simon Welch got in June, 1799, £2. 10s. 4½d. November 15 the same year, 15s. was given to Isaac Smith when he left the house. Peter Marsh of Greenfield in Shakerley took a boy, Richard Hampson, from the workhouse in 1801 and undertook to teach him weaving. John Barrat and James Arrowsmith, overseers of the poor, assigned him, and Mark Scholfield, the governor, was a witness. The agreed wages for the apprentice were 6d. a year, payable on Christmas Day, and only then if asked for them.

A Bombardier at Aboukir Bay, 1798

William Parkinson was born at Parr Brow and during the wars of the French Revolution he enlisted in the Royal Artillery. He was sent to Egypt and took part in the battle of Aboukir Bay, in 1798, when the British general, Sir Ralph Abercrombie, was killed. He saw active service throughout the whole of the Peninsular Campaigns and was never once wounded. When peace came to Europe after 1815 Parkinson was discharged and granted a small pension. This he had to eke out with handloom weaving. He died at Mosley Common, June 4, 1844.

Shakerley Colliery, 1798

This colliery was located between Higher Oak and Common Fold. It was existent and flourishing in 1798, for John Hope of Chaddock Hall had an interest in it, which he left to his son, John, and his son-in-law, Thomas Smith, with a right of pre-emption should either wish to dispose of his share. In 1825 James Overall was the agent for the colliery. He was living at Higher Oak in 1838. When in 1836 Jacob Fletcher purchased the Shakerley estates he acquired the mine as well, for his executors are rated for it in 1838. Its rateable value was £216. In 1853 Nathan Eckersley was the owner. He was uncle to William Ramsden. The remoteness of the colliery was the cause of the making of the road to Atherton across Shakerley, known as the old toll-bar road. As it was private property tolls were demanded from those who used the road as the shortest route to Bolton.

The Decline of the Shakerley Nail Trade, c. 1800

Baines says that the American War of Independence adversely affected the prosperity of the nail trade. Demand fell off and the manufacture was transferred to Staffordshire. The industry revived during the Napoleonic Wars. During the period 1820–40 there were still nailors in Shakerley; the marriage registers of St. George's reveal a stray nailor coming in an odd year to be married. But times were worsening for them, and in April, 1839, a smithy was set up in the carthouses of Lowton workhouse " for the employment of poor nailors," who came mainly from the Atherton and Shakerley districts. The powerful rise of coal and cotton after 1840 made it more attractive for workers to earn their livelihood by a new allegiance rather than stay in a traditional line. The age-old art of nailmaking in Shakerley at the present time is wholly extinct: in Atherton its place has been inherited with the nut and bolt industry.

Davenport House, c. 1800

Close to Davenports was built about this time Davenport house; then a superior domicile for superior people. In 1825, Mrs. Ditchfield lived here and in 1838, Thomas Charlton. An area of some two-and-a-half Cheshire acres was put to the house. Much later in the same century Atherton Selby resided here, and in 1871 the first Wesleyan minister in Tyldesley, John Saul, took up the tenancy.

Pear Tree House, 1800

At the beginning of the 19th c. a farm of this name belonged to William Speakman and fronted to Mort Lane; it was nine Cheshire acres in size. Jane Speakman lived at it in 1838 and died there on November 18, 1849. She also owned Morts Farm, Mill Brow, the Lower Bank, and the Higher Bank, small freeholds of some four–six Cheshire acres. About the mid-century a substantial house behind a row of impressive beeches facing Sale Lane was built, and John Holland was living there in 1858. This house and the surrounding estates were purchased by John Brown, who died in 1878. His widow, Margaret, leased the lower seams of coal to the Tyldesley Coal Co. Ltd., whose company later acquired the Bank House farms. The last of the Browns to live in the great house was Fanny Brown, who died in 1935. Soon after, the buildings were demolished and the site re-developed.

Richard Haldane Bradshaw Acquires Chaddock Hall for the Bridgewater Trust, 1810

The Canal Duke died in 1803 and the vast estates were managed by Richard Haldane Bradshaw. For the better getting of coal Bradshaw purchased from Samuel Clowes, Broughton Hall, but then of Sprotborough Hall, Yorkshire, the leased estate of Chaddock and Booths, and that part of the Warrington School land which had been let in 1782. The conveyance was dated July 14, 1810, and the purchase price was £47,000. Chaddock then extended to 50 Cheshire acres; it included Oliversons and Coupes farms, Hampsons at Mosley Common, a smithy at Stirrup Brook, two pews in Astley Chapel and one in Leigh Church, and a chief rent of £1. 13s. 3d. At some time later than 1722 certain quit rents, part of the lordship of Tyldesley Manor assigned to Wardley, sold to Francis Sherrington, sold again in 1690 and 1722, had been acquired by the Clowes of Chaddock. The ownership of these rents gave a manorial dignity to Chaddock, and the conveyance of 1810 describes the capital messuage of Chaddock as " the manor, lordship and reputed lordship of Tyldesley." In that part of its beneficial rights included the old commuted services of those tenants, who formerly owed suit to Wardley, the claim to be regarded as a manor was justified. But the passage of time had rendered the great feudal services of escheat, wardship, marriage, and the boon days obsolete and the rents payable were low. The total sum of the old quit payments was 9s. 0½d. as it had been in 1722 on the sale to George Kenyon. The list in 1810 was:

	s.	d.
John Hampson for Stonehouse	3	4
William Speakman—Bankhouse	1	0
Mill Brow	0	2
Jennies	0	4
Guests	0	4
David Grundy—Turncrofte	0	2
Widow Marsh—Dennis	0	1
Isaac Grundy—Morts	0	1
Thomas Tyrer—Mans Cottages	2	0
Mr. Starkey for Cleworth Hall	0	0½
Frogat for Damhouse	1	0
Thomas Johnson, Esq.	0	6
	9	0½

69

The Wesley Chapel at Tyldesley, 1815

From Shakerley the Protestant dissenters established themselves in Tyldesley. Thomas Heywood certified the house as licensed on November 30, 1809. Two years earlier Edward Gibbins, a minister from Leigh, had preached in a large room belonging to Thomas Radcliffe in Well Street; from here they moved to Samuel Bradshaw's house in High Street, and for a while they are identified at Conick's Hole in Castle Street. There were two certifications in 1812, January 14 by Ralph Peters, and July 2 by George Baxter. The trustees of Tyldesley Chapel sometimes lent their building to the Wesleyan ministers for charity sermons and from collections came the funds necessary to support their growing Sunday School. By 1815 they felt so strong that they built a chapel in Lower Elliott Street. The rent for the site was £2 per annum and the cost of the building £800. It seated 400, and Cawley and Burgess, cotton spinners of Tyldesley, subscribed £100 towards expenses. Attached to the chapel was a burial space: Sarah Rigby was the first interred on August 17, 1816. This first chapel served the connexion to the the year 1864, when it was enlarged: a collection in 1865 to defray part of the total cost of £1,300 realised £149. A school room was built at this time. This building in 11 years had become too small and had to be enlarged at an additional cost of £816. There were then some 500 Sunday School scholars. The earliest Wesleyan minister in Tyldesley was the Rev. Dr. Saul; he died in 1878 and was the first to be buried in Hough Lane Cemetery. The second chapel was replaced by a third, which dates from 1885, when both school and chapel were further enlarged at a grand cost of £4,100.

A Squatter on the Common, 1816

James Smith was a squatter on Shakerley Little Common; it is said that he built his habitation of turf sods in a night and continued to inhabit it for the necessary minimum period required by the custom of the locality. When his prescriptive title was complete he built a better house of brick and incorporated in it a window from the old Wesleyan Chapel. Neighbours referred to the house as Sod Hall, and for better differentiation James Smith and all the family were known as James Sod. There was half a statute acre of land attached to the " hall." Joseph Unsworth died at Sod Hall in 1887, aged 78. The place now no longer exists.

70

Around Factory Street there had, towards the close of the 18th century, developed a district, which from the number of spinning and weaving sheds was known to the folk of that day as New Mills. Messrs. J. and G. Jones were the master spinners, who directed the fluctuating fortunes of these satanic structures; they were harassed by industrial strikes in 1823 and 1826. By-and-by in the close neighbourhood other sheds were erected to share in the fabulous prosperity of this great era. Samuel Wilson, the builder of Hindsford House, managed one in Castle Street, this was successful and in 1836 Joseph Wilson built a similar mill in James Street. Later on Thomas Clegg acquired it; he raised it a storey higher and built a new part. The undertaking was known in 1853 as Hope Mill. In Baines's list of 1825 Charles Allcock appears as manager, resident at New Mills in that year.

Mosley Common School, 1822

A school was built at Mosley Common in 1822; there were trustees appointed and the building was sometimes used as a day school. A small cottage adjoined the main room for the occupancy of the master, and Thomas Longshaw tenanted it in 1838. J. Williamson was the last headmaster of this old school, which was pulled down in 1881 to allow for the building of the present one. Arthur Higson was the headteacher, who continued to the year 1921, when William J. Catchpole took charge. This school has recently been modernised to satisfy present-day needs and to cope with the growing population of Mosley Common.

Thomas Kearsley, 1823

Thomas Kearsley took a leading part in the affairs of his day and generation. He was a cotton spinner and in 1823 erected his Resolution Mill at a cost of £5,000; this prospered and in 1824 and 1826 he built two others, so that the combined blocks were shaped like a capital " L " parallel to Union and Ellesmere Streets. Kearsley lived at Fulwell, and in 1825 with Samuel Part built the Star and Garter. The Resolution Mills in 1838 were by far the most important and the highest rated. Kearsley owned other properties Nuttalls; five cottages in Elliott Street; five in Milk Street; two in High Street; and a house, stable, and slaughter-house in Shuttle Street. From the Shakerley estate he rented Brindles, Martins, and Cromptons Farms, which in 1838 had no dwellinghouses, but only outbuildings. In 1825 Kearsley laid the foundation stone of St. George's, where in 1828 he was churchwarden. Before 1847 he had ceased to be identified with either Fulwell or the Resolution Mills; in that year the factories were controlled by Jackson, Bayley. and Knott, and Jackson was living at Fulwell.

71

Tyldesley House, 1823

This commodious home in Davenport Fold was erected in the late 18th century by Thomas Johnson, the grandson, who lived here to the year 1823. George Ormerod, the historian, was with his uncle for a time. Baines gives him in 1825 as of Tyldesley House, and distinguishes him as Esq., Ll.D., F.R.S., and S.A. The historian's second son, George Wareing Ormerod was born here in October, 1810. He became B.A. of Brasenose, Oxford, in 1833, and practised as a solicitor. He died a bachelor at Teignmouth in Devon in 1891.

Laurel House, 1824

Laurel House in 1824 was tenanted by William Higson, who died there on March 2, 1836. Two years later William Halliwell was farming its 12 Cheshire acres. Thomas B. W. Sanderson, J.P., of Laburnum House, Atherton, was the owner. John Holland of the Tyldesley Coal Co. went to live there to the date of his death, when Dr. John Thomas Hobson became resident. He was followed by Thomas Carr (1873), Ebenezer Hobbs (1887), and for a period in this present century William Robert Smith.

The Blue Bell, 1824

When Baines, the historian of the county of Lancaster, compiled his directory in this year, the hostelry of the Blue Bell was standing in Sale Lane. Robert Taylor was the landlord. By 1838 it had changed its name to the Red Lion; George Barnes was tenant, John Ratcliffe owned it and the rateable value was £40, and in 1845 Joseph Dickens was the occupant; he was succeeded by Thomas Warburton, who occurs in 1858 and 1864. Warburton's widow was still here in 1881. With the turn of the next century there was John Morris (1909) and Fred Bannister (1918), licensees of this ancient staging inn.

The King's Arms, 1824

The King's Arms was built in 1823 by Messrs. Jones, the cotton spinners of New Mills, and opened on April 10, 1824. John Sutcliffe was first landlord; he was still host in 1838, by which year James Burton and Sons had acquired ownership. John Hodgkinson died at the inn in 1841. In 1847 there was Joseph Cunliffe. He died in 1852 and his widow, Sarah, carried on to her death in December, 1853. Thomas Sharp followed her, and in 1864, James Charlton. The inn became the property of John Burton, who sold it to George Arnold Mort, formerly a teacher at Tyldesley Church School. Mort brewed his own ale in Alfred Street. He died June 11, 1890, at the early age of 49, and on August 6 the premises were auctioned and acquired by Threlfall's brewery for £7,600. Joseph Bates was the landlord in 1918 and William Bates in 1924.

Bank House, 1825

Bank House stood opposite to Common Lane and after Well Street represented the earliest development of building on the Banks.

72

The house was of a type built to the taste of the new industrial magnate class and was a rival in Sale Lane of Fulwell in Squire's Lane. William McClure lived here; he was a fustian manufacturer who built his warehouses in the rear. The house possessed seven Cheshire acres and its rateable value was £83. Besides the warehouses, there was a barn, shippon, stable, and carthouse. At a later date, George Green of Yew Tree Colliery lived at Bank House, and in 1881 Owen Davies, minister of the Congregationalists.

Chaddock Lane Farm, 1825

Miles Arrowsmith, a manufacturer of cord, quilting, and Indian jeans lived here, and died here on October 7, 1839, aged 73. He was tenant of Lord Francis Egerton. The farm then had 13 Cheshire acres. In 1847 Peggy Arrowsmith had the farm and William Smith the cottage, which stood at the entrance to Park Lane. There were two other cottages on the opposite side of Chaddock Lane tenanted in the same year by William Hope and Richard Fish. In this century William Parker and William Peter Unsworth have been farmers.

The Spinners Arms, 1825

The great rise of the cotton industry was the cause of the creation of this old inn with its distinctive name. In 1825 it stood in Elliott Street next to High Street, and Thomas Manley was tenant. In 1838 the inn had a bowling green and its gross rateable value was £44. Charles Willott was owner and John Pendlebury, tenant. Two years later Francis Atkin had bought the inn and Thomas Guest was living at it to 1843, when he died. Ann Guest passed the Spinners Arms to William Hilton, who was here in 1845 and 1853. Then it changed its name to the Queens. William Lewis was landlord in 1881 and Samuel Cocker in 1890.

The Church of St. George, 1825

As a result of the victory over Napoleon, Parliament set aside substantial sums of money for the pious purpose of building churches in areas where the thrust of population had made the provision of new and adequate spiritual facilities a necessity. It was fitting in these circumstances that the dedication should go in honour of the national saint. Thomas Johnson gave the site in 1820, and the first stone of this new daughter church of Leigh was set in position by Thomas Kearsley of Fulwell House, on April 23, 1822. The church was designed by Sir Robert Smirke, R.A., and consecrated by Charles James Blomfield, Bishop of Chester, on September 19, 1825. The Commissioners for Erecting National Churches granted a sum of £17,000 and the deficiency was made up by George Ormerod. Ormerod enlarged the original site given by his uncle; he gave £2,000 towards the cost of walling in the burial ground; he bought the organ, he installed the bells, and bought the communion plate, Bible, prayer book, and the chancel window. The first curate was Jacob Robson, B.D., who held the office to the year of his death in 1851. He came from Leigh Church to Tyldesley. The church accommodated 1,100, its length is 112 feet, width 60 feet, the height of the nave 45 feet, and that of the aisles 30 feet. The spire, a local landmark, is 150 feet high.

The Queen's Arms in Chaddock Lane, 1825

Baines calls this once lonely inn of the great turnpike road the Queen's Head, when he listed it in 1825. Richard Smith was the tenant. In 1838 it is new styled the Queen Anne, with Lord Francis Egerton as proprietor, and a high rateable value of £152. It possessed then its own brewhouse, and Smith farmed Oliver Fold land as well. James Harrison occurs in 1847 as landlord, Thomas Cockshout in 1873, Charles Frow in 1909, and William Weedall in 1918 and 1924.

The Star and Garter, 1825

Tyldesley's most centrally situated hotel dates from 1825, when George Ormerod leased to Thomas Kearsley, of Fulwell, and Samuel Part a plot of land from his " Bancks " estate. At the time of the lease Ormerod was living at Welbeck St., Cavendish Square, London. The rent reserved as first chief by the Star and Garter lease was £63. 10s. per annum. Samuel Part was the first tenant. There was a bowling green to the rear of the house, and a garden. Ralph Ainsworth was the host in 1838, and Kearsley still the owner. Its gross assessment for rates was £66. The bowling green along Shuttle Street is shown in 1848. The local justices used to hold their sessions here. Colonel Ross, of Astley Hall, and John Jackson, of Fulwell, jurisdicted at the Star and Garter in 1848. On Kearsley's death, Nathan Eckersley became owner, and William Robinson was tenant in 1847. Then Henry Howarth in 1853 and 1856. Henry Grindrod was both auctioneer and licensee in 1858. Thomas Smith had the hotel in 1865 and 1869, William Crook in 1871, and John Valentine in 1873. James Holland was licensee for a time before John Mee. In 1883 the Stouts began their long association with this hotel. Henry Stout came in that year, and his son, Thomas, prolonged the tenancy to the year 1927.

The Bells of Tyldesley, 1825

The bells of Tyldesley—the gift of a great county historian—were cast in 1825. The rim inscriptions are:

1. Long live King George IV. 2. Give no offence to the Church. 3. 1825. 4. William Dobson, founder, Downham, Norfolk, 1825. 5. Prosperity to the village of Tyldesley. 6. These bells were cast by William Dobson, Downham, 1825. They were brought on August 10, 1825, from Leigh to Tyldesley, each bell drawn on a

cart by three horses, which appropriate to the day and occasion had jingling bells affixed to their collars. The carillon was in 1910 increased to eight bells and at the same time they were all rehung. For many years now Tyldesley bells have joyfully summoned the living to worship and have tolled in muffled muted measure for the committal of the faithful. So vigorously did the bellringers in vicar Lund's day draw the ropes that the clangour disturbed the service in the Wesleyan chapel, which began half an hour earlier in the morning. A protest was made and an arrangement agreed which was satisfactory to both. In 1925 James and Robert Allred had been ringers for 45 successive years, and a grand peal of 5,056 changes was on this landmark occasion rung in their deserved honour.

Chaddock Lane Colliery, 1826

A coal pit was once located to the south of Engine Row; in 1838 it was the largest concern in the township, being rated at £780. Most likely it was first sunk by the Duke of Bridgewater sometime in the 18th century. In 1828 his agent, Richard Haldane Bradshaw, was said to have spent £10,000 on plant. Moses Bury was for 15 years an overlooker at these pits. Bradshaw worked the seams on lease to the late Duke; he bought out the interest of Clowes in the Warrington School land and he tried to acquire the fee simple from the trustees, but did not succeed. He paid to them for the period 1807–17, £1,100 royalties; in 1824 for the years 1821–23, £398, and for the years 1825–6, £997. These large sums are an indication of the rise in capital values of Sir Thomas Boteler's original endowment of the school. The colliery was still working in 1848.

The Delph Mills, 1826

In the Delph, the natural frontier of the vills of Tyldesley and Worsley, where for centuries the Roman urns lay buried from the light of day, stood originally a windmill to grind the corn. In the great era of power looms cloth displaced wheat as a source of profit. J. Smith was a manufacturer of Chaddock Hall, who had some interest in this old Delph Mill. Thomas Smith, who lived at the New House in 1826, added a new shed to accommodate 200 looms, and the valuation of 1838 gives Robert Smith and Brothers as the owners. There was then the windmill, corn mill, old cotton mill, new cotton mill, warehouse, shop, sowplace, taking-in room, power loom shop, gas works, engine house, and boiler house, all assessed at £322. By 1847 the firm had divided; Thomas had the old windmill and Robert the cotton mill and lodge. Philip Manley was owner sometime before 1869. Thomas Silcock followed on in 1871. He manufactured jute, bags, and sackings. He built a row of cottages known as Silcock's Row. The Delph Mills were demolished in 1893.

St. George's School, 1827

Subscriptions were raised in 1827 to provide for the erection of a school, and a site was given by George Ormerod; for many years members of the Ormerod family were trustees of the foundation. Boys were taught in one part of the school and girls in the other. In 1853 Peter Bent was headteacher and Sarah, his wife, was in charge of the girls. Such an arrangement must have proved workable, but when both headteachers were not joined in the harmony of matrimony friction often arose. An assistant and two pupil teachers usually helped the headmaster and sometimes paid monitors taught. In 1859 Moses Molyneux was head, and in 1863 the average roll-call was 154. Molyneux taught to the year 1868. In 1864 Archdeacon Ormerod and Henry Mere Ormerod came to inspect the school as trustees. Molyneux's relations with vicar Richards were not always happy and when one of his managers, Dr. Hoyle, spoke to the boys in school one day and got no obedient response, he likened his order to " a rope of sand." The Burtons, especially Oliver, took a great interest in the school, and Edward was for a long time treasurer. In 1868 John Best became master; he was very conscientious and died of overstrain, in 1872, at the early age of 37. James Longstaffe was elected to succeed him; he was soon at loggerheads with the mistress of the girls; she engaged in active conspiracy to effect his dismissal. In 1873 only 54 boys came to the school and in December, 1874, the managers terminated his services. From 1875-90 John Grounds taught, he recovered some of the lost prosperity and its numbers in 1897 rose to 179. During Ground's office, the weekly instruction fee was raised to 4d. . Henry Kirkpatrick had succeeded Edward Burton as treasurer in the school and there is a note of February 1, 1877, when he showed his magic lantern, then something of a new wonder, to the boys. William Ramsden was a good supporter of the school as manager, and at Christmas it was his custom to send each boy a small gift. When in 1890 William Pinnington was appointed, the attendance was the highest on record. The Congregational School in High Street had closed and accommodation was so restricted that no further boys could be taken on. There were then five staff; one, Louisa Pemberton, was the first woman teacher of the boys. It was at this time that Fred Burton defrayed the entire cost of a new infants' school, and soon the managers and congregation had to bestir themselves to cope with the problem by building an entire new school in the eastern part of the township.

James Burton comes to Tyldesley, 1828

James Burton was born at Clitheroe in 1784; he was one destined to play a great part in the development of industrial Tyldesley. His working life, first began with the firm of Thompson, Chippendale and Co., which he left to come to Tyldesley in 1828, where at the age

76

BURTON HOUSE AND BURTON MILLS, DEMOLISHED 1926

of 44 he entered into partnership with John Jones and Richard Jenning Jones of New Mills. Messrs. Jones were more interested in silk weaving and finally moved away to Bedford, leaving Burton in sole control. By 1838 he was well established and the firm of Messrs. Burtons owned extensive properties in the western part of the township. In this year he was living in Charles Street in a house rated at £25, in the midst of his workpeople. In and around Charles Street and Castle Street Messrs. Burtons owned 74 cottages and 57 cellars, as well as a house in Elliott Street, and the King's Arms at the corner of Castle Street and Charles Street. Families lived in the cellars below ground level as well as small trade artisans. In 1839 Burton crossed Shakerley Brook and built Atherton Mill: on the near edge of the boundary of Tyldesley and Hindsford was the gasometer to give light over the machines on winter working days. According to a trade directory of 1845 Burton had taken in partners, for his firm was then styled Burton, Chippendale and Co. This association was later dissolved, and as James Burton and Sons the company became one of the most extensive undertakings of its day. Before he died in 1868 three other mills had been erected, Lodge Mill (1853),

Field Mill (1856), and Westfield (1860), and all were in production. Burton took little interest in politics, though he was a Liberal. He was quiet and unassuming. For many years he represented his adopted town on the Board of Guardians, and became its chairman. He was succeeded in the control of the mills by his sons Oliver and Fred. The latter when he died was virtually a millionaire. On November 14, 1883, there was a great fire at Burtons Mills, which caused £15,000 damage. In the 1920 boom the mills were over capitalised and in the great depression the buildings were stripped of all their machinery and demolished. James Burton is buried in St. George's Churchyard.

The House in the Square, 1828

Three years after the building of the Star and Garter, James Newton took a lease from George Ormerod of a plot called the Strutts and built thereon a typical 19th century house. Newton was a corn dealer and in his time the post-chaises and horse diligences pulled up at the George and Dragon, on their diverse routes to Leigh, Manchester, or Bolton. For him it was a convenient place. He died in 1852 and his executors were Thomas Kirkpatrick, cotton spinner, and William Hesketh, grocer, both of Tyldesley. On Newton's death the house was tenanted by a surgeon and in this way began a century's association with medical practitioners, who in manifold ways have served the township. The first was William Hoyle, who acquired the interest in the lease from Newton's son in 1866. Hoyle died in 1886, and his signet ring was incorporated in a part of his memorial erected in the Church of St. George. When his daughter Edith died at Woodhall Spa in 1918 she left £2,550, subject to life interests in favour of Mrs. and Miss S. H. Sunderland, to Tyldesley church for the curate's fund and for the repair of the fabric. Upon Hoyle's death the next surgeon was Dr. Dixon: then came two brothers Harry and Edward Hamer. When Harry died the brother carried on the extensive practice, and in 1919 he bought the house in the square from Miss Sunderland. He retired to live in Norwich, and in 1925 sold his residence to Dr. Andrew Bury, who as physician, lived here to the year 1951. On the site of this house stood the original fish stone stalls set up by Thomas Johnson in 1782.

Richard Haldane Bradshaw Buys Garratt Hall, 1829

The trustees of the great Duke of Bridgewater in this year bought Garratt Hall from the Rev. Thomas Clowes of Darlaston Hall in Staffordshire, to whom it had come by way of inheritance. The price paid was £21,000. The Bridgewater Estates Ltd. are now the

The Sale of the Shakerley Estate, 1836

The Shakerleys continued their very old tenure of the hamlet to this year, when it was auctioned at Tyldesley. The personal ties of the family with Shakerley had become very slight. Peter Shakerley gave two guineas towards the rebuilding of Leigh Grammar School in 1719. In 1836 the estate was for sale. The details describe it as the Manor or reputed Manor of Shakerley cum Tyldesley, co. Lancs., with various farms and lands in the township, containing together 514 acres of land statute measure: and the valuable mines of coal and stone lying under the same; the yearly chief rents of £1. 13s. 4d., and certain pews in Leigh Parish Church. These properties were praised for their advantageous position, lying four miles from Bolton, and one from Leigh: the land of excellent quality, tithe free; the estates abounded with thriving young timber; the mines of coal were inexhaustible, of excellent quality, and being in a manufacturing district found a ready sale which would be vastly increased if the projected North Line of Railroad betwixt Liverpool and Manchester be proceeded with. The purchaser was Jacob Fletcher, of Peel Hall in Little Hulton. He died soon after, and his only heiress was a daughter, Charlotte Ann. She married in 1866 Robert Wellington, 3rd Viscount Combermere, from whom she was later divorced. Her second husband was Major Stapleton-Corrie.

Minister Langridge and the Church Rate, 1837

When Tyldesley obtained its own established church in 1825, by law the churchwardens became empowered to levy a rate on all except empty properties to cover the incidental and needful expenses of the church. Such items, according to the accounts, covered repairs to the fabric, binding of the Bible, new bell ropes, glazing of windows, payments to the bellringers, fire in the vestry, the cost of communion bread and wine, expenses of attending visitations, colour washing and cleaning the church, ironing the vicar's surplice, and paying the sexton to ring the bell at 8 o'clock. The rate varied from $\frac{1}{2}$d. to 1d.; its highest was in 1833 at $2\frac{1}{4}$d. The rate was compulsory to the year 1857, when it became a voluntary rate. Its yield at $\frac{1}{2}$d. in 1842 was £24. 10s. $5\frac{3}{4}$d., and at $1\frac{1}{2}$d. in 1846, £75. 6s. 7d. Such a tax was obviously unpopular with dissenters. Minister John Langridge of Top Chapel at the public vestry of April, 1837, opposed the levy and demanded a poll of all the ratepayers. The result: 226 in favour of the rate, 186 against. Langridge failed to carry his victory home.

Richard Worthington, 1831

The Worthingtons were a modest and small manufacturing family of Mosley Common; they appear quite early in Tyldesley industrial history. The Commercial Directory of 1816 gives R. Worthington of Tyldesley as a dimity and quilting manufacturer, who attended to meet his customers at 7, Baileys Court, in Manchester. Richard Worthington died May 13, 1861, aged 83. He built his mill in 1831; it was a weaving shed holding about 60 pairs of looms, later enlarged. Roger Worthington was his son. In 1878 the mill was the property of James Cooke. Later it passed into the possession of the Applebys, who used the premises for the manufacture of soap. The building stood originally on the roadside opposite to the King William Inn. There was a bowling green and meadow attached to the mill, which in honour of the Prince Consort was called the Albert Mill. Richard Worthington lived at Mosley House. His son, Roger, was one of the members of the Local Board in 1863. The mill was damaged by fire, March 30, 1858, and Peter Hampson was their manager for many years.

Barlow House, 1828

The year of building this house in Lower Elliott Street is said to be in 1828. Sometimes the name is given as Barton House, from the family who once lived there. Henry Barton, a cotton spinner, was resident here in 1847. Eliza Barton died June 10, 1853, and was buried at St. George's. Samuel Gee Taylor had the house and its spacious gardens in 1864 and was still here in 1872. He was a member of the firm, Clare, Taylor and Co., who had the Hope Mill. In 1888 Mrs. Taylor and Miss Taylor gave vicar Lund a donation of £20 towards the restoration of the church. The house was demolished to make a site for the new board school, now the Girls' Senior School, in 1913.

City Pit, 1838

The Bridgewater Trustees were operating this colliery in 1838 when it was rated at £253. Thomas Hall lost his life here by firedamp, 1843, and James Edge, by a fall of roof, 1858. City Pit was sometimes known as Gatley Pit and was still winding coal in 1880. The Ellesmeres, who succeeded to the City Pit, moved their main shafts to a site near the Ellenbrook on the border of Tyldesley and Worsley. Here in 1872 they commenced sinkings and the group of pits now known as Mosley Common Collieries began its industrial life. Gatley is still a place name in the City.

Old Hatters, 1838

Old Hatters, a quaint name, was the designation of a farm north of Cleworth Hall, it was sometimes known as Randle Smiths. Peter Makin occupied it in 1838 and John Redford had the cottage. Its area was 12 Cheshire acres. John Makin died here, May 25, 1847: his widow, Nancy, farmed the land for a time. Peter Kerfoot was here in 1864 and 1873.

Moss Farm, 1838

Moss Farm, now derelict, was for a long time the habitat of the Summerfield family, who have left their name in local topography in the lane which climbs the Banks. In 1838 Lord Francis Egerton owned it and James Summerfield farmed its 18 Cheshire acres. The farm and field names betray the existence of the mossland at the foot of the Banks. Two of its closes are called the Yarn Croft and the Yarn Croft Top, for yarn was a rough weed which stubbled the pasture.

Shakerley New Hall, 1838

Shakerley New Hall was built almost in the curtilage of the Old Hall. It had originally no land assigned to it. In 1838 it was occupied by John Guest and Thomas Battersby. Thomas Kearsley, the cotton spinner, rented Shakerley Old Hall, but he let off most of the land to Crompton Farm, which stood in Common Lane. John Crompton had been tenant of the Old Hall in 1824, and in 1853 John Leigh was living there. He was still tenant in 1873. Thomas Wharmby then followed.

At the Sign of the Boar's Head, 1838

At the top of Castle Street there once stood this inn, its site is now an open space. It was of a later date than the Flaming Castle. In 1838 Wilderspool Brewery controlled it and Sarah Ratcliffe was their tenant. By 1853 Samuel Howarth was licensee; he was followed by his son Jesse, who died in 1889. John Pendlebury was licensee in 1909.

Mill Brow, 1838

A small holding which lay to the north of Turncroft, and which was the freehold in 1838 of William Speakman, was Mill Brow. Jeremiah Hampson of Stonehouse took the land and let the house to James Eckersley. Its individual extent was six Cheshire acres. Isaac Grundy lived at Mill Brow, where he died, September 4, 1829. Later, Lot Lomas is located here. Then Eckersley died January 8, 1841, and in 1873 William Gillibrand was tenant-farmer.

Paddock's Pit, 1838

This colliery was the smallest of the five pits raising coal in 1838. George Grundy and Co. were the owners and its value for rates was £144. It was still winding in 1846, when Francis Adina Grundy was killed in the workings. The shaft was in Makant's Lane, just north of the farm.

Old Fold, 1838

On the waste edge of Mosley Common originally stood Old Fold; it was part of the endowment of Ellenbrook Chapel, and Samuel Grundy was trustees' tenant; its area was some 23 Cheshire acres. In 1838 no farmhouse was in existence, the survey of 1848 shows several buildings of the fold standing, and in this century died here Ellen Gillibrand (February 1, 1840), Peter Edge (January 8, 1844), Thomas Greenhalgh (July 28, 1851, aged 80), and Martha Lunn (June 5, 1854, aged 54).

Warrington School Estates, 1838

Kearsley's valuation of this year shows that from the year 1828 there had been little change in the value of the Warrington School Estate. The New House, which finds a mention in the report of 1828, stood along Mosley Common Road and was occupied then by Thomas Smith. Andrew Howarth died there December 30, 1856. Grundy's farm, so called in 1782, had as tenant in 1838 Richard Smith, and Urmstons in the same year Nathan Dunster. The combined gross rateable value of these properties was £180.

The Shakerleys Ennobled, 1838

Geoffrey Shakerley, the royalist, who died in 1696, was succeeded by his eldest son, Peter, who died without issue, and the estates passed to a half-brother, George, who besides his Hulme properties bought land at Gwersyllt in Denbigh. Peter, his second son, followed on and from him the family traditions passed to a daughter, Eliza, who married Charles Buckworth. Their heir, Charles Watkin John, of Somerford Park, assumed by Act of Parliament the arms and name of Shakerley in 1788, and was High Sheriff of Cheshire in 1791. His eldest son, Charles Peter, disposed of the ancient hamlet of Shakerley in 1836, and two years later was created a baronet. His heir was his son, Charles Watkin Shakerley, born in 1833, and like his grandfather he became High Sheriff of the County Palatine of Cheshire in 1863. From him the present holder of the title, Sir Cyril Holland Shakerley, is descended.

Ranters Chapel at Mosley Common, 1838

The Primitive Methodists established an early foothold in New Manchester, and from the connexion formed there grew the present chapel. Long before they were strong enough to boast a building of their own, the Primitive brethren rented a small cottage from Fanny Worthington; it was listed in the valuation of 1838 as Ranters Chapel, and the evidence is that there was no day tenant in the cottage, but that it was used exclusive to their worship. The present chapel dates from 1868, and in 1907 a centenary memorial new Sunday School was built.

Shakerley Toll Bar, 1840

The cobblestone road that led right across Shakerley to Greenfield was a private road constructed in the 19th century, and the use of which, except to the farmers of Shakerley, was subject to tolls. The origin of the road lay in the need to get coals by land sales easily away from the collieries in Shakerley. In 1864 a board was exhibited at the bar detailing all the charges payable for carts, horses, and cattle. Kine, sheep, and pigs were reckoned in scores. With the decline and disappearance of the coal mines in this area the significance of the road went as well, and in 1949 only 2s. 6d. was collected in an entire year. During the last century the Kays were for a long time toll bar keepers. Thomas Gibbons was the last: he had been there some 40 years since 1909.

Roger Tyson, 1840

The first post office in Tyldesley was in Castle Street, from here it migrated to a shop near the Boar's Head, then to the Flaming Castle, then to Alfred Street, and finally, for the last century it has been in Elliott Street. Roger Tyson was postmaster in Alfred Street when Sir Rowland Hill introduced his universal penny postage. Though only a penny to frank a letter the addressees had personally to call at the office for any letters, otherwise a charge of ½d. to 2d. was made as extra for delivery. Tyson died August 23, 1858. William Higson succeeded; he ran a printing business along with Mackenzie, to cater for the needs of those people who wanted bills and posters. It was during his time that post office savings bank was attached to the branch at Tyldesley. Higson moved the office into Elliott Street, he died at the age of 45, on July 8, 1872, and his widow, Betsy, carried on. She was followed by Matthew Hunter, who served the township from his shop at the top of Lemon Street. In 1890 came John Kershaw, who moved the office to 137, Elliott Street. He retired in 1918, and from that year to 1950 Mrs. Ada Holland was postmistress. Since this latter date there have been two postmasters, L. Stonier and L. Davemport. The office is now a Crown office.

Mechanics Institute, 1842

It was in the year 1842 that pioneers in democratic education set up a Mechanics Institute. The aim of these early founders was to augment the education of apprentices and mechanics engaged in industry, and instruction in a wide range of technical subjects was provided. The treasurer of the institution in 1845 was Peter Unsworth, in 1851 the secretary was Peter Bromley and the treasurer John Unsworth. In 1853 Caleb Wright was secretary; Thomas Syms, treasurer; and Joseph Higginson, headmaster. Prizes were given from subscribed funds, and Caleb distributed these on one occasion, October 14, 1886. William Lomax, who lived in Meanley Street, describes himself in 1881 as Secretary of the Temperance and Education Hall. During the day time Wilfred Dean Stone kept a private school in the institute in 1887. Charles Russell Croft was headmaster in 1890. Much of the educational work of the institute has been inherited by the Technical School. In 1908 the Mechanics Institute at Tyldesley ceased its useful life; it was wound up and its assets conveyed to the town council. On its site was built the present library.

Barnfield Mills, 1844

Just as Kearsley created Resolution Mill and Burton the Hindsford Mills, so did Caleb Wright lay the foundations of Barnfield Mills. It was in this year that H. P. Barton and Caleb Wright, in partnership, built their first mill in Union Street. Wright had leased the field known as Barnfield from the executors of Peter Eckersley. Before 1866 Barton had disappeared, for Wright had at this time Peter and Charles Eckersley as partners. Together they launched the second mill. In 1870 the firm was known as Caleb Wright and Co., when a third mill was ready for spinning. Three other mills were later built, and after the death of Wright, the entire undertaking was absorbed by the Fine Spinners Combine. In 1890 Thomas Hamer was secretary.

Tyldesley Coal Co., 1845

George Green's pit, after many disappointments, caught up with prosperity. An authorisation ticket for a sheet of iron to be delivered to Peter Greenhalgh, written out by Green himself in 1849, gives the principals at that date as Green, Leigh, and Cowburn. The company deepened its shafts and extended its lower surface extractions by additional leases and other sinkings. On Shakerley Common a pit was sunk which had the first iron headgear in the country. This finished working in 1878. In that year the Combermere started; this was closed in 1896. In 1882 Peelwood began to wind and continued operative to 1928. Owing to a fault in the strata it became necessary to sink another shaft in order to win the near-surface seams. This pit was known as the Daisy Pit. The company came on the Starkie Hall estate in 1874. When the Eccles to Wigan railway was opened in 1864 the colliery constructed a siding on to the main line. In 1870 the company became limited in liability. Its output of coal in 1871 was 25·825 tons; it reached its highest in 1907 at 419·471 tons, and in 1920 it was returned at 267·848 tons. On December 11, 1858, there occurred a firedamp explosion at Yew Tree Colliery, when 25 lives were lost; 14 of the victims were buried in St. George's Churchyard. George Green died in 1886, at Wharton House, Ellesmere Park, Eccles. James Bridge was secretary of the company in 1887, and James Atherton mining engineer.

The Clock in the Spire, 1847

The church clock was paid for by public subscription in 1847, the cost was £200. In time this clock became worn out and Henry Kirkpatrick paid for a new one at his own costs. The congregation of the church bore the charges for repairs and sometimes an outsider, like Charles Eckersley, realising the benefit which it bestowed on young going to school and those who were older passing by to tram and train, sent his donation of three guineas towards keeping it in good condition. In 1912 it was agreed that this responsibility should pass to the town council; the township at large pays for the illumination of the dials and the repairs, and since that date the clock of St. George's has told the hours by night as well as by day. A new agreement was made in 1937, when electricity superseded gas as the method of lighting up the four faces.

Tyldesley Tithes, 1847

The tithes payable on the various fields of Tyldesley had experienced a chequered devolution since the time of the Reformation. In 1838 they were valued at £80. 13s. 6d. for the year, and the impropriators were Jacob Fletcher's executors. A full enquiry was made in 1847, and it was then disclosed that the tithes of corn, grain, and pulse were merged in Shakerley Manor, and altogether the tithes in Tyldesley issued out of 1,695 acres of meadow, 350 acres of arable, and 40 acres of common. The trustees of Ellis Fletcher took in 1847 £61. 12s. 11d., Lord Francis Egerton received for Garratt Hall's 330 acres £16. 10s., and John Farnworth for his six acres in the tenancy of Richard Grundy 12s. Additional to these lay-impropriated sums was a payment of £30 made annually to the perpetual curate of St. Helens. These tithe payments varied according to the fluctuation of price and harvest, and were based on a seven years' average. In some cases to avoid uncertainty the payment had become fixed by custom, and in Tyldesley for each calving cow 2d. tithe was paid in lieu of tithes of milk and calves; 1½d. for each barren cow for the agistment of cows; 1s. for each colt; and 2s. 6d. for each litter of pigs; 1d. for each hive of bees in place of the tithe of honey and wax; 4d. on each acre of meadowland for the hay, lamb wool, and pasturage; and 1s. for each flock of geese to represent the tithe on poultry. Most of the cottages and buildings in Tyldesley paid a small tithe of a few coppers, made in apportionment as the town grew and developed. The cost of collection was heavy and in this present century the whole payment of tithes has been abolished by commutation. Capital sums were assessed to be paid to extinguish these charges on the land, which in course of time had diminished so much in value.

Hursts, Shakerley, 1847

The heretic of 1558 and the webster of 1606 were memorialised by this farmstead in Shakerley. Thomas Hurst in 1606 had rented a field from William Turton of Turton Fold, and Hursts was part of the Shakerley estate. Ellin Hurst, spinster, died in 1684; she left legacies to eight of the children of Richard Hurst, and her estate of £91. 13s. 6d. was divided substantially between Thomas and John Hurst and Ann Asherwood of Harwood in Bolton. By 1838 Hursts had been detached from the Shakerley estate; its house and two Cheshire acres belonged to Wharton Hall and Joseph Lever was tenant.

Astley and Tyldesley Coal Co., 1847

This company had pits in both Astley and Tyldesley. One mine was working in 1847 when John Darlington was getting minerals under Astley Hall land. Quite near were other old shafts on Meanley's farm. The company changed its corporate name several times: at first it was known as Astley and Bedford Collieries, Leigh, with offices at Bedford Lodge: later, it was styled the Astley and Tyldesley Coal and Salt Co. Ltd. Samuel Jackson was owner in 1856, followed by Henry Jackson. The company eventually comprised St. George's Pit (Back o'th Church), Gin Pit, Nook, and Kermishaw. In 1869 the secretary of the company committed fraud and was sentenced to five years' penal servitude for embezzlement. The location of the collieries explains the rise of Gin Pits as a district remote at that time from either of the two township centres. The company built many houses to accommodate the workers, some of whom had migrated from Staffordshire, and Peace Street, Maden Street, Lord Street, derive their names from former directors, who were once actively engaged in building up the prosperity of the concern. By a lease of 1857 the company agreed to pay the lessors of Astley Hall a minimum annual rent of £1,000, and royalties as for the Binn mine £70 per foot thick per Cheshire acre, for the Crombouke £95, the Brassey £70, and the Six Feet £95. The lease was to expire in 1896. To the year 1889, when Astley Hall estate was sold, Astley and Tyldesley Collieries had paid for these mines and the Worsley Four Feet in royalties £90,526. The lower mines, the Seven Feet and the Trencherbone, were not included in the lease of 1857. For 46 years John Walshaw was manager. Thomas Smith, of the Lingards, Astley, later became managing director. R. G. Green was in charge of Nook Pit, 1888-98.

The Hearse House, 1847

Adjacent to the Flaming Castle, and conveniently located for its purpose, was the hearse house. The churchwardens were the persons charged with the expenses of maintenance and taxes. The house was rented in 1849 from James Summerfield, annual rent £2. 2s. Then it was acquired by Mr. Crank, who had his pew rent of £1. 1s. deducted from the same sum payable to him. The rates and taxes were: 9d. small tithe, 5d. gas rate, and 1s. 6d. to 1s. 9d. poor rate. The house was evidently taken over about 1847, for in that year Thomas Sharples made the hearse at a cost of £42. Besides the coach itself there was the harness and saddlery. This was damaged in 1852 and William Antrobus, a local saddler, repaired it. By 1858, after 10 years' wear, the plumes were shabby and George Grindle charged £5 for doing them up. In 1852 the driver was supplied with a cloak, cost £1. 10s. and bought off Thomas Gerrard. There are items of expense for repairs to the coach in 1859, and to the harness in 1860. By 1859 Henry Andrews had bought this strange house of sad utility.

Burgess Colliery, 1848

This small colliery was existent in 1847, and the mound of shale visible to-day from Stonehouse is evidence of its former activity. Mrs. Burgess was the owner of the land and James Atkin lessee of her minerals.

Boothstown Wesleyan School, 1849

Methodism took ready root at Boothstown, and a Wesleyan Sunday School began here in 1849. Its convenience soon established it as a day school and additional space was provided in 1881. August, 1884, saw these premises opened as a separate school, with George Deddow as first headmaster. He left in 1902 and was followed by William Haughton, who died six weeks later. Elijah Spencer taught from 1902 to 1926 when William Garnett was appointed. From 1936 to his death in 1952 H. Hagerty was headteacher. Guy Rowson, one of the Tyldesley born Members of Parliament came from this school.

Tyldesley Co-operative Society, 1850

The phenomenal success of the Rochdale Equitable Pioneers, who set up a co-operative trading association in 1844, was the cause of many similar ventures being floated in various parts of

Lancashire. Tyldesley Co-operative Society opened its first shop in High Street, April 16, 1850, and was then called the Tyldesley Commercial Co-operative Society. The founders met with success, and using the capital of purchasing members they bought in January, 1861, a shop and three cottages from Joseph Harwood, for £760, which were situate in Shuttle Street. In 1864 the concern was known as the Tyldesley Co-operative Provision Society. The prosperity which had aided the new society in 1850 was not sustained, and on August 17, 1864, Tyldesley was in such difficulties that it sought to escape them by becoming absorbed in the more efficiently managed Leigh Friendly Co-operative. There were some 200 members and after negotiations had at first fallen through, in October, 1865, Leigh Friendly took over the Shuttle Street shops, which they still control. James Dickinson was the first manager; he was dismissed by the Society, and William Johnson followed. In 1885 the Tyldesley and District Industrial Co-operative Society began modestly in a building opposite to the present central premises, now occupied by Isherwoods. R. F. Unsworth was part-time secretary in 1894, and from 1900–1904 Arthur Boardman was full-time. This second association prospered and there are now 12 branch shops serving the township and immediate districts: from a membership of 1,000 in 1900 there are now over 6,000. Thomas Markland has been secretary since 1919 and general manager from 1934. Besides Leigh Friendly there are two other societies which trade within the township—Hindsford and Atherton at Shakerley, and Walkden Provident Industrial at Mosley Common.

The Old House in Alma Street

_ This small holding, once part of the Ormerod lands, covered seven Cheshire acres in 1838, when it was farmed by Joseph Cottom, who was still here in 1847. Its historic name has been forgotten, but it is now called Bank House. Development has taken much of the meadow and pasture on which its prosperity once rested. In 1838 besides its shippon and barn there was a cowhouse in the meadow.

The Public Library, 1851

On the site of the library in Stanley Street was originally the Temperance Hall and Mechanics Institute, which dates its existence from this year. Caleb Wright laid the first stone. William Lomax was one of its enthusiastic promoters, and John Buckley was for a time secretary of the Temperance Society. The hall cost £550 and was used not only for occasional meetings, but for organised classes as well. In this way arose the Mechanics Institute and a library of several hundred volumes was got together. It is recorded that the Institute library had 400 volumes in 1856. In 1908 the Town Council took advantage of the terms of a Carnegie grant to erect a more

TEMPERANCE AND EDUCATION HALL, DEMOLISHED 1908

imposing building and to provide a public library, the collection
formed by the Mechanics Institute and the Tyldesley Co-operative
Society being utilised as a nucleus. On December 18, 1909, Charles
Eckersley performed the opening ceremony. Harold Holker was
the first librarian from 1909 to 1920. He was followed by William
Eckersley, who retired in 1952.

Reeds and Healds, 1853

The great rise and industrialisation of the cotton trade in
Tyldesley caused two brothers, Ellis and Thomas Dean, to begin
the manufacture of reeds and healds for looms in a small shed to
the rear of Barlow House. By 1853 they were well established and
later moved their works to its present site in Lower Elliott Street.
Thomas died in 1885, and Deãn Villa in Upper George Street is
commemorative of the family name. Ellis left no issue, but a
namesake son of Thomas succeeded to the business, which at the
present day is managed by the grandsons.

Wesley Chapel, Boothstown, 1853

The Methodist enthusiasts, who began a Sunday school and day school in Boothstown, became more and more desirous of building a chapel. Funds were collected and one erected; it was first opened on October 14, 1853. The following Sunday great sermons were preachéd and collections made, which realised £60. This first chapel continued in use to the year 1872, when the present building replaced the earlier one on the same corner site.

Tyldesley Wesleyan School, 1856

The old 1815 Wesley Chapel with its brick floors, central pews, and spacious sides, where on great occasions forms were placed, served from at least 1856 as a day school. The building was heated by a large stove on that side where the girls were taught. The first masters were: William Henry, Joseph Storey, Joseph Hime, Joseph Veal, and Mr. Taylor; and Cecilia Miller and Clara Bayley were early girls' teachers. In 1859 a small addition was made, which served as extra space for the growing school. This proved inadequate and in 1864 a new school was built; at the same time the chapel was enlarged. In 1870 the day school passed under the supervision of the State. Later, in 1880, further alterations were made to the day school and J. M. Ely was appointed head-master, with Mary Moscrop as infants' mistress. There were then some 500 scholars. Ely taught to the year 1912, when the school ceased to exist. In 1885 an entirely new school was built for the reception of an ever increasing number of day scholars, computed at that time to number 650. Even this did not solve the difficulty, and the trustees purchased the adjacent house, the White House, in the garden of which they built a new wing to provide for the infants. This school did great work in its day; it succumbed because it could not cope with the financial demands made on it to maintain an ever higher standard of accommodation set by those rival schools which leaned on the support of the State.

The Sexton, 1857

The ancient sexton of St. George's Church had a variety of duties to perform. He took orders for burials, he kept the church-yard in good repair, he locked the church and the yard gates, he tolled the bell on specified days, he kept the register of graves, he dusted every week and cleaned the church thrice a year, he was in sole charge of the firewood and brushes. He was expected to hold his office with sobriety, reverence, and respect, and draw his wages of £5 per annum. When the clock was installed he secured the extra-duty of winding it and oiling it, which brought him in an additional £2 a year. Richard, Daniel, and John Sixsmith, of the old Shakerley family of that name, were first sextons. Afterwards there came William Higson and Edward Bowker.

Canonbury House, 1853

Lieutenant John Hine is located at Canonbury House in 1853 and died there in 1865. James Knott, a cotton spinner, followed, and on his death, in 1872, William Duncan, a medical practitioner, took up residence. The house passed into the ownership of Thomas Smith, who let it to tenants. Robert Isherwood spent the last few months of his life here and his son, Fred, succeeding him, died at Canonbury House in 1950. Robert Isherwood was treasurer of the Lancashire and Cheshire Miners Federation. His activities made him typical of his day, for he took a great part in trying to conciliate the conflicting interests of capital and labour, so acerbated by the chronic strikes of the 19th century. Seeing that the miners had no place to meet and assemble for mutual benefit, he conceived the plan of erecting a hall. Miners' Hall was completed in 1893. Robert Isherwood died in January, 1905.

The Primitive Methodist Chapel, 1859

From New Manchester the Primitive brethren came in 1856 to Union Street, where they hired a room, held their services, and supported a Sunday school. In 1859 they built their chapel in Shuttle Street at a cost of £350. By 1875 they had outgrown their restricted accommodation, and in that year the chapel was enlarged to seat 250 and a new school erected. For a time W. D. Stones was headmaster of the day school attached to this chapel, and Emily L. Stones, head of the infants. This Primitive Methodist school was closed at the same time as the Wesleyan in George Street, and the scholars transferred to the new Elliott Street Council School. Stones became a teacher here. He died July 26, 1916, aged 57.

Parr Bridge Mill, 1859

Parr Bridge Mill inherits the tradition and skill of those early weavers in that locality, whose cloth, yarn, size, and tow formed such important items of their personal wealth. The mill was built in 1859 and in 1865 was owned by Richard Farnworth. Four years later John Jackson was proprietor. In 1872 appears Jones and Co., their warehouse was at 19, Fountain Street in Manchester. By 1876 the mill had been purchased by William Porritt, who moved his finished stock to 7, New Brown Street, Manchester. In 1879 Samuel J. Middleton owned it; he was a contributor to the building of St. John's Church opposite. Later, the Forsyth Bros. acquired the mill. It was idle for some years before 1920, when the present firm of Robert Farnworth Ltd., of Bolton, took over. The mill specialises in weaving rayon dress fabrics and has been converted to electric power driving.

Peter Bent, 1860

Peter was most likely the first master of the boys at the national school, and his wife, Sarah, was his counterpart with the girls. He was a man of many parts and duties. For in addition to teaching, he was parish clerk. He signed the church accounts in 1840 and in 1851 was paid 7s. 3d. for copying registers. When the churchwardens set up the hearse house, Peter, who lived next door but one to the Flaming Castle, very near to the hearse itself, was put in charge of all matters pertaining to its financial side, its repairs and its hire. He had to collect all the charges, and in 1860 was paid 7s. for his trouble. His most lucrative side-line was washing the vicar's surplice. His bill, paid out of the church rate for this, was 13s. in 1842, 15s. 2d. in 1844, 19s. 5½d. in 1851, and in 1853 £1. 17s. 4d. He died June 4, 1864, and Mrs. Hatton in 1863 took over the washing of the surplice and the church linen.

Local Elections, October, 1863

By 1861 the population of the township had doubled since 1801 and was still on a rapid increase. The old parochial semi-manorial framework of local government was creaking in the strain of a new industrial age, and in 1863 the township decided to adopt the powers conferred' on it by the first Local Government Act of 1858. On October 24, 1863, was elected the first council of a new authority styled then the Tyldesley Local Board; it contained famous names, men representative of the best elements the neighbourhood could produce like Caleb Wright, Oliver Burton, William Ramsden, and George Green. Tories mixed with Liberals, master spinners, and colliery proprietors, types of a new merchant society, which in wealth, ability, and sagacity had long ousted the entrenched landed classes. This local board met its problems with considerable courage, and from its deliberations devolved immense benefit for the generations which came after. It took over the operation of the Gas Works in 1865 from a private company, and in 1876 built the Union Street Baths. In 1879 it purchased the burial lands of the cemetery, and in 1884 completed the Morley Hall Sewage Works. But all these improvements which marched steadily in the social status of the township aroused then bitter opposition and violent controversy.

Township Government, 1863-1953

The early council met in Lower Elliott Street opposite to the Fire Station. Amos Cranshaw was first clerk and surveyor. He died in 1891; from that year to 1901 Frank T. Wright was part-time clerk with a full-time deputy in Henry Morris. There were two assistants at this period, Addin Tyldesley and Percy Martin.

On Wright's resignation in 1901, William James Matthews, coming from Luton, was chosen as successor. Matthews, who lived at Mosley House, and later at Hill Crest, died in 1933. The clerkship then passed to John Robert Cockfield, who resigned in 1936. A solicitor, M. W. Coupe, followed to the year 1939 when R. F. Wilson took up office. John Brooke Smith was first separate surveyor; this office from between the years 1911–42 was filled by F. E. Jones. Philip Lyon, John Anderson, and Albert Davenport have acted in succession as accountants. The great diversity of delegated duties and the onerous responsibility of housing have during this century advanced the importance of the council to a point hardly visualised in 1863. The great achievements of township government in the present era have been the creation of Astley Street Park, the building of the library, the development of housing estates in Sale Lane, Mosley Common, and Shakerley, and the making of a through road to Blackmoor, developments which, judged by capital outlay, dwarf completely the record of the latter half of the 19th century as represented by the baths, sewage, gas works, and cemetery.

PLOUGHING IN CROSS FIELD, TYLDESLEY, 1850

The Railway, 1864

A railway was spoken of for Tyldesley many years before actual construction. The Lancashire and Yorkshire Company first obtained powers to proceed with a track joining Eccles and Wigan and passing through Tyldesley, but the time limit imposed expired. In 1861 the London and North Western Company revived these powers and on Sept. 11, 1861, the Earl of Ellesmere cut the first sod at Worsley. The line was declared open for traffic on August 25, 1864, amid great rejoicings. In 1880 the Hough Lane bridge was found unsafe to carry the roadway above the line; it was blown up and a more substantial one set to replace it. Thomas Kniveton was the first stationmaster.

Mrs. Richards, wife of the vicar of Tyldesley, was crossing the line, before the making of the subway, when a train ran into her and severed her leg completely. This was on June 14, 1871. Another accident occurred at the junction with Green's siding on December 16, 1878. No one was killed, but the main line was blocked for three hours. Some 20 people were injured, among them being Charles Eckersley's wife, Jane, and Dr. Hewlett of Astley.

Formerly there was a separate master for the goods station.

Grundy's Patent Heating Apparatus, 1864

John Grundy was a grocer who served in his shop in Elliott Street; the District Bank now stands on the site. He worshipped in Top Chapel where he was warden. Both chapel and shop were cold to his feet in winter, and he pondered long how to overcome his discomfiture. At last an idea came to him and he asked permission to experiment in heating the chapel from the convenient school room below. He succeeded and in his stove, flues, and ventilators, all working in combination, he made an apparatus for central heating. He took out successive patents and constantly improved the efficiency of his invention. Later, a more convenient vehicle for heat was found in water and to-day the company, which he established, makes central heating stoves, pipes, and radiators for all types of buildings. The firm has specialised in the heating of churches and one of the many, where their system is installed, is the church of the Holy Trinity at Stratford on Avon. Grundy, the founder, died in 1893 and to-day his firm are general ironfounders with works in Lower Elliott Street.

Morecambe Sands, 1865

Three sons of James Charlton, landlord of the King's Arms in Tyldesley, had on June 22, 1865, been on a trip to Windermere. Daniel Charlton was a B.A. of St. John's College, Cambridge, his brother, James, was still an undergraduate there, and Henry, the youngest, was barely sixteen. They all alighted at Hest Bank intending to walk on the shore back to Morecambe, where they were on holiday. The tide cut them off; Daniel and Henry in trying to escape sank in the quicksands. James took a different route and climbed the bank to safety. The bodies were later recovered and buried in St. George's churchyard.

Water, 1867

An expanding town needed a good supply of water independent of Shakerley Brook and the numerous wells, which had for centuries supplied groups of cottages. The elders of the council of 1863 had long been faced with this great problem, and to solve it they turned to the springs in Cutacre Clough. Long ponderous debates were made on the sufficiency of this supply and the qualities of the water it could produce. The proposal to build a reservoir and tap this natural source was shelved on the question of annual cost. Instead, application was made to the City of Manchester for a supply, and Tyldesley in 1867 made an agreement with that authority for a fixed quantity of water to be supplied weekly. In 1893 Astley township was supplied with water by Tyldesley for a period to expire after 30 years. In 1903 Tyldesley had to make a new agreement with Manchester for additional quantities to meet the needs of expansion and growth, steadily taking place. When the 1893 agreement ended in 1923, Astley obtained water direct from Manchester: the amalgamation of Tyldesley and Astley in 1933 complicated these arrangements for the supply of a natural element, without which the two townships under modern conditions could not continue for long to function.

The availability of water, constant and under pressure, made it possible for it to flow up through pipes and to be laid on to houses in any room. This pressure enabled fire brigades to operate with greater mastery over that ever present danger to industry and life. Tyldesley in 1865 had its fire engine, which Matthew Owen kept in readiness in Castle Street. By 1879 the brigade was stationed in Lower Elliott Street. Captain Darlington was the superintendent. The same supply led to agitation for public baths. The controversy in the council chamber extended to convulse the whole township and there arose two bitter camps, the pro- and the anti-baths. Eventually the cause of progress triumphed and in 1876 the Union Street Swimming Baths were declared open.

William Ramsden Disappears, 1869

William Ramsden inherited the Shakerley Colliery from his uncle, Nathan Eckersley. In 1869, at the age of 35, when he was sinking another pit, the Nelson, things were going badly for him and he disappeared for a while from the local scene. His action caused a stir and Hewlett, vicar of Astley, in his diary makes these two entries: Tuesday, March 23rd. William Ramsden, coal proprietor of Tyldesley, has not been seen since last Friday, when he went to the Bank at Bolton, or rather set to go, for they have ascertained he has not been. Monday, May 17th. William Ramsden made his appearance at one of the collieries at a very early hour, having it is said, walked from Liverpool. He has been in Ireland all the time; his friends have been racked with anxiety about him.

Ramsden had married the daughter of William Hesketh, who in 1838 lived in a shop in Elliott Street, owned by Jeremiah Hampson, the site of which is now Barclays Bank. She was a sensible woman and faced with the dilemma of no husband, men's wages to pay, and collieries to keep working, she approached George Green of Yew Tree Colliery and asked him to help with his experience, until the situation cleared. No doubt acute shortage of money was the cause of Ramsden's disappearance. But in the end he made good and served the township of Tyldesley with commendable ability for 25 years. He was first elected to the local board in 1863 and with Caleb Wright was chiefly responsible for pushing forward the building of the baths, which had caused so much opposition in the town. As chairman of the gas and water committee it fell to him to lay the beginnings of the gas undertaking. He was a loyal supporter of Tyldesley Church, and in his memory the eagle lectern was given. For 20 years he was president of the Conservative Club. He left Guest Fold in 1898 to retire into Herefordshire, where at Hampton Bishop he died in 1904. His wife died in the same year, three months earlier.

A Nocturnal Burial, January 18, 1870

Suicides were buried at crossroads in ground unconsecrated. A kinder view prevailed when John Hope took his own life. He was buried at midnight, the hour of zero, on January 18, 1870, in St. George's Churchyard. No service was permitted to be said over him, as his body slid into the dark hole. The coroner had found that he had causelessly circumvented his own existence; stigmatised to the bitter end, he was buried by lanthorn and sped on to join the unblest company of Ophelia.

96

The Congregational Chapel, 1870

The Congregationalists built their chapel in High Street; it cost £2,300 and was opened by the Rev. Enoch Mellor, D.D., of Halifax, August 18, 1870. Previously, the congregation had met in the Temperance Hall, where William Hope Dawson had begun services in 1866. Funds were collected in 1869 by means of a bazaar, under George Green's patronage, to build the chapel in High Street. There is accommodation for 450. In 1871 a day school was begun. The pastor, Joseph Robert Webster, taught the children at first, but in the same year Henry Clayton became master. An early minister was Edmund Daniels. The opening of this school had the effect of enticing scholars away from other places, especially half-timers, who found the afternoon session, which began at 2 p.m. in High Street, more convenient after working the morning shift. William Cooling was master of the boys from 1874 to the cessation in 1891. Emily L. Brown taught the girls. Another teacher was Kate King, who later married Thomas L. Syms. Charles R. Croft and Jonathan M. Ely were the first pupil teachers of this school. Of the pastors—Joseph Cockram served from 1873–1880; he left for Garstang and had lived at New Bank House. Owen Davies was his successor. S. D. Martin resigned in 1936 and William Lawson in 1941.

John Holland, 1871

Holland came into Tyldesley from Ireland, where as a railway contractor he constructed the first railway there. On his taking up a share in the management in the Yew Tree Colliery, he brought all his gear and equipment to Tyldesley, where it littered the yards of George Green's pits. Holland who was a staunch Catholic had three sons, William, James, and Ambrose. James became licensee of the Star and Garter, and as Catholics had no place to meet and worship in, James allowed them the free use of a loft. The great number of Irishmen who came to settle on the coalfields at this time influenced Tyldesley's growing population, and Lord Lilford was asked to donate a plot of his land in Chowbent to allow for the building of a church, school, and presbytery. This he did and in 1869 the church of the Sacred Heart at Hindsford was dedicated. John Holland materially helped on the building of the church by giving all the sand, mortar, and bricks that were needed. He died two years later. His son, James, formed a romantic attachment for one of his barmaids, eloped with her and crossed over to the States.

97

Johnson Street School, 1871

It was during the time of vicar Richards that this school was built for the convenience of parents dwelling in the east end. The growth of Tyldesley at this time was peculiar; it tended to leave the industrial region round the church and to spread itself eastwards, and this was its direction of expansion for many years. The Johnson Street site was acquired for some £300, and the school built soon after was, according to the trust deed, for the education of children and adults or children only of the labouring, manufacturing, and other poor classes in Tyldesley, and for no other purpose.

The school opened on January 8, 1872, with 38 children, and Sarah J. Hargreaves was first headteacher. There is a record of 1889 which states that a Mrs. Berry took her son away and sent him to a school where boys did not learn sewing. The numbers steadily increased until in 1897 there were 189 registered on the books. In that year the three permanent teachers were assisted by two pupil teachers. The capitation grant per scholar in 1901 was 17s., which brought in a State subsidy of £125. 16s. to meet some of the expenses of the school. Modern electric lighting was installed in 1938.

New Lester Colliery, 1872

New Lester Pit stood near to Makants in Mort Lane. Its business name was James Roscoe and Sons. The colliery owed its existence to the drive of Roscoe, who once worked as a miner in one of the old pits in North Lane. He left his employment to go on the railway and at Leicester he became head of the locomotive department. The application of more up-to-date means of getting coal convinced him that a new mine in Mort Lane to tap the deep lying seams would prove successful, though this area had shown many old shafts, which the labour of early generations had abandoned. He was right and in 1872, with the money he had saved and in partnership with William Roscoe he began his new Lester Pit, so called because he left Leicester to come back to Tyldesley. His first home was at Park House, Astley, where he lived 10 years, and here he became a great admirer of Dr. Hewlett, though himself a Primitive Methodist. He laid the foundation stone of the Primitive Methodist Chapel in Tyldesley. In 1890 he died at Kenyon Peel Hall and was succeeded in the management of his colliery by his two sons, Thomas and George. Thomas married Catherine S. Hampson, of Astley, in 1900; they lived at Kenyon Peel as tenants of Lord Kenyon. Later, Thomas retired to Aylesbury in Bucks., where he died in 1926. The colliery as an output unit ceased in 1941.

George Ormerod, 1873

The historian and antiquarian of the City and County of Cheshire died in 1873. He was born in High Street, Manchester, in 1785, and went to the King's School, Chester—hence his early interest in the city. When the master, the Rev. Thomas Bancroft, left to become Vicar of Bolton le Moors, Ormerod followed him and was his private boarded pupil. He entered Brasenose College and graduated B.A. in 1803; M.A., 1807; D.C.L., 1818; and F.R.S., 1819. He succeeded to the Banks estate on the death of his uncle, Thomas Johnson. In 1811 he purchased an estate at Chorlton, in the parish of Backford, Cheshire, and later bought Sedbury Park, Gloucestershire, where he lived for many years. From 1813–19 he was engaged on writing his history of the County Palatine of Chester, a magistral work on which his fame to-day chiefly rests. It was issued in three volumes, a revised edition appeared after his death. Ormerod left a large family of seven sons and three daughters. His eldest son, Thomas Johnson Ormerod was a scholar and fellow of Brasenose and an authority on Hebrew and Semitic languages. The great historian became blind in his later years.

**GEORGE ORMEROD
DIED 1873
CHESHIRE HISTORIAN
GAVE TO ST. GEORGE'S CHURCH
THE ORGAN, BELLS,
COMMUNION PLATE AND
CHURCHYARD WALL**

Banks, 1873

Industry in Tyldesley led to the rise of the banks. In 1870 William Ramsden was using a bank at Bolton, and soon after the Union Bank of Manchester set up a branch in Wareing Street, and later at 147, Elliott Street, which was managed for a long time by Henry Brown. Cheques were drawn on Glyn Mills. William Redfern succeeded Brown and managed both the branches at Leigh and Tyldesley. William Bentley committed fraud, which obliged him to serve a prison sentence. Fred Isherwood in 1908 began his long association with the bank and retired in 1933. Milnes then followed, whose life was cut short by an accident with a revolver in 1940. By 1890 two other banks had set up in the town. One was the Bank of Bolton, in Stanley Street, under Thomas Pickering, and the other, the Consolidated Bank of Manchester, in Lower Elliott Street, under the agent, Thomas Cotton. The Bank of Bolton later became the Manchester and County Bank, now the District Bank in Elliott Street, and the Consolidated Bank was known as Parr's Bank and is now the Westminster Bank with premises at the top of High Street. The Union Bank of Manchester in course of time established sub-branches at Astley and Boothstown, and in 1940 amalgamated with Barclays group.

The Square, 1877

When Thomas Johnson gave a piece of Crossfield for the erection of Top Chapel the boundary on the north side was set back some distance from the highway, with the idea of allowing access of the carriages of the genteel, who resorted there. In 1825 his nephew leased the land on the other side of the highway for the building of the Star and Garter. A similar provision for the post coaches caused this inn to be well set back from Elliott Street, but the land remained private property. In time, as the township grew this open space proved convenient for a market place for all the neighbourhood. People came from afar off to show their wares and were ready to pay a rent for the privilege of opening out a stall, quite apart from the fee charged for the hire of the stall itself and light in winter. In time an inevitable conflict of rights arose. On September 12, 1877, the Council bought from Rev. G. T. B. Ormerod the area in front of the chapel and the hotel. A right over an area of six yards wide along the Star and Garter and the house in the square was reserved to these two properties by the deed. The next year the local board claimed jurisdiction over the market place and issued summonses against the owners of stalls, which were not authorised by them. The licensee of the hotel had let the area over which he had rights of access and collected the rent. The dispute went to Kirkdale Sessions: the local board lost the day; they appealed and the appeal was dismissed. In 1880 an agreement was drawn up by which the licensee of the Star could collect all toll from the market stall holders at a fixed rental of £30, which he had to pay to the Council each year. This was a compromise, which worked well during the years that followed.

Private Adventure Schools, 1877

During the 19 c. several schools were established in Tyldesley which were sometimes styled academies, boarding schools, or dames schools. Tyldesley had no free school of its own until 1822, though some of its poor children were admitted to Astley Mort's school. In 1825 there was a school in Davenport Fold run by James Halliwell: its tradition persisted and was inherited by Mrs. Davies's Dames School in 1880, which was located in Davenport House: the daughters of the Wesleyan Minister, Dr. Saul, helped with this school. J.

Constantine managed another academy at New Mills and Richard Lythgoe one at Mosley Common in 1825. The Mosley Common School was still functioning in 1853 under James Lythgoe. In this year Miss Eliza Gretton had a boarding school at New Bank House. She left here to go to Chaddock Hall, where she maintained, about 1877, a girls' school of a high reputation, which was well supported by the better class of the neighbourhood. Hewlett, vicar of Astley, sent his daughters there and Miss Hayes is the sole name of any scholar which has been handed down of all those who once went to this vanished Victorian finishing school for young ladies at Chaddock Hall. Elizabeth Atkins's academy was in Astley Street between the years 1856 and 1865. Betsy C. Holland was also a private teacher in 1856. William P. Mann's school was in Elliott Street in 1865, and in 1879 Wilfred Stones began the building up of a good local private school, which met and assembled in the Temperance Hall. The New Bank House School was managed in 1887 by Mrs. Baxendale and the Misses Mather.

The Welsh Calvinistic Chapel, 1878

When many Tyldesley pits were being sunk to win from nature her hidden riches, different nationalities flocked into Tyldesley. Welsh folk left their hills to follow their colonist relatives and became so numerous that they congregated together to worship in their own faith and tongue. In the early days different creeds combined for community worship in the Wesleyan day school and made little of their differences: Methodists and Baptists prayed and sang together. In time came the desire to possess a chapel, and the insistence of the Baptists to incorporate a baptistry caused a split. Two chapels arose, one in Shuttle Street and the other in Milk Street. The first Welsh Methodist Chapel, built of wood in 1878, was replaced in 1903 by a brick building.

Morley Hall, 1880

In this year Tyldesley Council purchased from Peter Warburton, G. B. Gregory, and Ann Wilkinson, one half of Morley Hall. By a strange historic turn of events the townspeople of Tyldesley acquired a moiety of an ancient hall, which from 1564 to 1755 had been part of the possessions of the Tyldesley family. James Tyldesley of Holcroft in the latter year had conveyed to the Leghs of Chorley the whole of the Morley estate, and from them one half came to Josiah Wilkinson, then to his son, John Wilkinson, of Southampton, who made his will in 1816 and ultimately to the vendors, who concurred in the sale of 1880. The other half passed to Thomas Lyon of Warrington and has come by various mesne dealings to the National Coal Board. The rapid expansion of Tyldesley had made the need of a sewage system imperative and the natural gravitation from the Banks to Morley and the nearness of the estate to the Glaze combined in commending the purchase as ideal for its purpose. The price paid was £12,500.

Strikers Attack Wharton Hall Colliery, February, 1881

Wharton Hall, outside the township limits, had 18 Cheshire acres within Tyldesley. The Hall was for a long time the home of the Morts; the last of the male line, Adam, had two daughters who married Thomas Earle and Richard Gwillym. These sold in 1870 the estate to John Gerrard Potter who formed the Wharton Hall Collieries. There was a gas explosion at this pit in 1877, and in 1879 James Beswick was their manager. In the great strike of 1881 strikers from all over the neighbourhood marched on Wharton Hall Colliery to bring out the blackleg workers. Extra reinforcements of police from the county were drafted to protect the plant, and in a baton charge, Sam Findley, of Atherton, lost his life trying to escape a frontal attack made to disperse the crowd.

The Liberal Club and the Town Hall, 1881

The two great Parliamentary Parties of the 19th century set up substantial buildings as club premises to which they transferred their members. It was on January 6, 1881, that the Liberals saw their new headquarters completed at the top of Well Street. Caleb Wright, assisted by Charles Eckersley, performed the opening ceremony, and there were then some 400 members. A year earlier the Conservatives had launched a similar project; they built their hall on land rear of the Star and Garter, and like the rival club, the building served as party centre. It was here on September 7 during the election campaign of 1885 that Lees Knowles spoke at a meeting under the chairmanship of William Ramsden. Whereas to-day the Conservative Club still functions, the fortunes of the Liberal Club declined with those of the party, and in the early 20th century the membership dropped so much that the club could not carry on. The building, however, took up a new lease of life and purpose, for it was taken over as a town hall and seat of local government. It was in 1924 that Tyldesley Council acquired the beneficial interest in the premises for £2,000.

Original lease, April 2, 1880, G. T. B. Ormerod to Owen Borsay, ironmonger, and John Mather, pawnbroker, both of Elliott Street; rent of £23. C. Wright advanced £1,000 in 1888 on mortgage, which was repaid to his personal representative in 1901. A builder, Robert Latham Martland, took a sub lease of a strip of land at a rent of £6 in 1884. This was assigned in 1894 to Joseph Wallwork. This property had a right of way to the rear, which was surrendered in 1949.

John Mee and the Teetotallers, 1881

Mee was landlord of the Star and Garter. In this year the Sons of Temperance and the Water Drinkers held a propaganda and crusading meeting on the Square at his very doorstep. This was too much for him. He issued forth and approached the speakers, pointing out that they were on private property and asked for the usual toll charge. The Sons of Temperance were indignant and refused to pay. Mee was determined: pay or go off. They paid and the meeting carried on.

Thomas Kirkpatrick, November, 1881

Kirkpatrick, like Caleb Wright, was once apprentice to Messrs. J. and G. Jones of New Mills, Tyldesley. He was born in 1806, and has so prospered that in 1845 he was able to buy Hindsford Mill near to Shakerley Brook. He lived for a time at the Walmesleys in Bedford, but later purchased Meanleys as a residence, and in 1864 acquired another mill at Hindley Green. Kirkpatrick was a Liberal; he sat on the township councils of Tyldesley and Bedford and was for twelve years chairman of the Leigh Board of Guardians. At his death he left four sons, Edward, Henry, James, and John, and a daughter, Annie, who had married Caleb Wright. He died November 19, 1881. Though the Kirkpatricks never operated on the same extensive scale as their rival contemporaries in the cotton trade, they were a constant force for good in the neighbourhood and made their influence widely felt throughout two long generations.

St. John, the Evangelist, Mosley Common, 1885

On St. Valentine's Day in 1885 Katherine Louisa, Countess of Ellesmere, laid the foundation stone of this granddaughter church of the parish of Leigh. From the early years of the 19th century, services had been held at Mosley Common in the school, and this mission was directed from the nearby chapel of Ellenbrook. The growing population pressed on the need of a better and more suitable building, and in 1885 various subscribers gave sums of money towards the £4,250 which the church cost. The Bridgewater trustees donated the site, and the Earl gave £500 to the building fund. Lord Lilford another £150; Mrs. Harrison of Chaddock Hall, £100; Henry Yates, of Rydal Mount, £100; and the bells were the gift of John Higham of Swinton. Because of the lack at first of an endowment fund the consecration was deferred to March 8, 1895, when the ceremony was performed by the Bishop of Manchester. The Earl of Ellesmere provided £1,000 towards the establishment of the endowment. Mrs. Brown of Pear Tree House gave the pulpit, Mrs. Higham the lectern, Mrs. Harrison the font, and Mrs. Whitehead the reredos in memory of Ellis Whitehead, the first organist. T. R. Pennington was first curate; he was succeeded by Joseph Morris in 1884, who was responsible for the present building. The church was raised to the dignity of a vicarage and made a separate parish in 1894. The first vicar lived at 36, Coupe Brow, near its crossing with the East Lancashire Road. This residence was gutted by fire, August 13, 1901, while the vicar and his family were on holiday in the Isle of Man, and the loss was the cause of the present house being built close to the church in 1905. Morris died April 11, 1905, at the age of 54, and was buried at St. Marks, Worsley. Matthew Hall was next vicar; he was tragically ill for many years and vicar by title only. A succession of curates carried on the active pastoral work of the parish until the last, Simmons, became third vicar on the death of Hall in 1929. Frank Simmons left in 1936, when Robert Kee was presented by the Bishop, who is patron of the living.

A Gladstonian Liberal, 1885

Caleb Wright was the most outstanding personality of that group, who during the progress of the 19th century did so much to advance the prosperity of Tyldesley.

He was born in 1810, one of a family of 13. On September 15, 1826, his father hired him for three years to spin with J. Jones of the firm which then owned mills in Hindsford. In afterlife the note, by which he was bound, became one of his treasured possessions. After 12 hours a day at work, he attended night classes and Sunday school and taught himself to read and figure. His father died in 1832 and he joined with his mother as breadwinner for the family. He left Burton Mills in 1841 to become manager of Ormerod and Hardcastle at Bolton, and while here attended Bolton Mechanics' Institute. In 1851 he entered into partnership with H. P. Barton, of Manchester, and built his first mill of 20,000 spindles. Wright was a Unitarian and a lover of music; he succeeded his father as organist at Chowbent Chapel and was himself a member of the Tyldesley String Band. His elder brother, John, a spinner at Burtons emigrated to the States and travelled as a musician in various parts of the world. He returned to Tyldesley about 1870. Wright's mill prospered and others were built, until finally, there was a group of six, with a pay-roll of 800. Caleb was living in 1853 at Hindsford House. He married June 15, 1859, Annie Kirkpatrick at Tyldesley Church. His son, Frank, in 1887 married Annie Eckersley of Fulwell, daughter of Charles Eckersley. In 1885 Wright was invited to stand as the candidate for the newly created Leigh division by the Liberal party. His Tory opponent was Lees Knowles and the poll, 4,261 for Wright, and 3,725 for Knowles. He fought altogether three elections and retired from the Commons after sitting as member for ten years at the great age of 85. Wright was a shrewd, slow speaker. In his day Disraeli was the champion of the Tories, and the primrose was Dizzi's favourite flower. In Leigh division were set up " primrose habitations " at various partisan houses, where from time to time the Primrose League met for social and political gatherings. One such habitation was at Astley Hall and another at Guest Fold, the home of William Ramsden. On one occasion, after a great meeting of the rivals, Wright quietly observed that "primroses would not grow in his division." Later history had demonstrated how absolutely true he was. In other respect Wright was farseeing; he supported home rule for Ireland and the extension of the franchise to women. This great local figure died April 28, 1898, at Lower Oak.

CALEB WRIGHT, M.P.,
GLADSTONIAN LIBERAL.
DIED APRIL 28, 1898

The Advowson of St. George's, 1888

The right of patronage to the parish church of St. George belonged as of right to Lord Lilford, for he was the lay impropriator of the rectory of Leigh, and Tyldesley was first a curacy, and later a vicarage carved out of the old parish of Leigh. Robson, Richardson, and Lund were all presented by Lord Lilford. In the year 1886 steps were taken to buy the advowson, the purchase price of which was agreed at £300. The advantage of acquiring the right of patronage and vesting it in the bishop of the diocese was that the Ecclesiastical Commissioners were prepared to augment the annual value of the living to £300. The parishioners set about to raise £100 by themselves and the remainder was given by outside friends. From this year the Bishop of Manchester has enjoyed the right of presenting the vicars of Tyldesley.

The Inquest at the Boar's Head, April, 1891

The Boar's Head Inn, which stood at the crest of Castle Street, saw 12 jurors headed by their foreman, Thomas Bentley, solemnly assemble in this month to enquire into a tragedy which had darkened the dark history of Burton's sombre mills. The weaving manager was Thomas L. Syms, who lived quite near, at 53, Castle Street, with his wife and three children. Burton's bookkeeper was Philip Hill, a bachelor, of 14, Ashwell Street, where he kept house with his sister. Both he and Syms had worked at these mills some 40 years apiece. Hill was a morose man, who nursed imaginary grievances and thought certain people shunned him. At ten minutes to seven on the morning of April 8, Syms was crossing the mill yard from Factory Street when Hill, agitated, met him and fired two bullets into his breast. Mary Ann Ainsworth, from her bedroom in Factory Street, saw the tragedy enacted before her very eyes. Hill then rushed into the building and blew his own brains out with the other two bullets in the revolver chamber. Syms was not dead, when discovered, but he died the same day in the kitchen of his own home. His namesake son in later life became a distinguished photographer; he was many years a councillor and was chief citizen in 1906-7 and from 1913-20.

The Burning of Resolution Mills, September 26, 1891

By 1853 James Bayley and James Knott had acquired control of Kearsley's Mills, the Resolution group. Bayley lived at Fulwell and was a magistrate. His wife's name was Ann. He died April 9, 1862, and his partner, Knott, died at Harrogate ten years later. Knott was then living at Cheetham Hill. In 1888 the children of James Bayley built the chancel and choir stalls as a memorial to him and his wife, who are buried in the churchyard. The firm still went by the name of Bayley and Knott, but sometime after 1880 Caleb Wright took directive control. On September 26, 1891—Wakes Saturday— Resolution Mills were burned to the ground. James Pasquill, an overlooker, first discovered the fire. The brigades from Tyldesley, Leigh, and Bolton rushed to put out the blaze but failed. The damage was estimated at some £30,000. This severe loss caused Caleb Wright to establish a fire service of his own for use on the premises, in case of further outbreak.

John Buckley, 1892

In very striking contrast to George Ormerod stands John Buckley, who in 1878 compiled a naïve account of his native Tyldesley, which, meritorious for the events of the 19th century, lies humbly outshone by the princely tomes of the landowner-historian, whose estates had been so enriched by the rapid industrialisation of Tyldesley that he was thereby enabled to undertake historical work with greater force and vigour over a wider stage and field. Ormerod was a doctor of Oxford and Fellow of the Royal Society; Buckley had not even 5s. spent on his education. The first writer on Tyldesley history was a member of the Top Chapel, and a Liberal: a founder of Tyldesley Mechanics Institute and a lover of animals. He died suddenly at Douglas, October 19, 1892, and left £200 to erect a drinking fountain for horses and cattle on the Square. Henry Mere Ormerod, a solicitor, of Stanley Street, for some obscure reason opposed the idea, but the fountain was eventually set up and stood for many years on the Chapel side.

When at last with the disappearance of cattle and horses its original utility was diminished, it was removed and rebuilt in Astley Street Park.

**JOHN BUCKLEY,
HISTORIAN OF TYLDESLEY.
DIED OCTOBER 19, 1892**

The Mission School, 1892

Restricted accommodation in the old National School and the dense population of Tyldesley in the east end created the urgent need of a new school. In this year arose the Mission School in Darlington Street. The aim of the early enthusiasts was dual in purpose—a school and mission combined. William Ramsden gave the land and on October 22 his wife laid the foundation stone on a rainy day, amidst a gathering of local clergy and notabilities. The cost of the building was £1,700: George Brown of Pear Tree House was the architect and Cockers of Walkden the contractors. Two of the early headteachers of the new school were Miss Showler of Leicester and Miss Buckley of Huddersfield. In 1896 another building, detached from the original mission, was erected in two storeys to cater for the growing population of scholars. In 1903 William Pinnington of the National School left to become head of the then more important Mission school. He remained to the date of his retirement in 1923. On his staff at that time was George Cook, who had been private secretary to the Earl of Ellesmere and had taught for many years in schools in India. He retired the same year. In 1925 Pinnington was appointed a manager of his old school; he died in January, 1927. His successor was George Smith, who in like manner, left the old National School for the

Mission. There were then some 500 scholars attending this school. Smith taught to the year 1934 when William Tyldesiey returned as head of the school, where in 1914 he had begun his career as a teacher. He stayed for a year and in 1935 left, when Roger Hosfield took charge. It was during his tenure of office that five of the Mission school scholars, all of the Tyrer family, were burnt to death at their home in Green Bank Street in the holocaust of the night of January 13, 1936. The Mission has been served by a succession of loyal and devoted teachers, among them was Miss Morris, who in 20 years was never once absent or late, and Miss B. Stones, who taught there for 42 years. Hosfield left the Mission in 1949 to become head of the reorganised junior school of St. George's. In the apse of the Mission are two stained glass memorials, one of William Ramsden and the other of John Kay, manager of his Wellington Pit, who was killed October 1, 1895, by an explosion of gas in a new airway.

1. Total cost £2,740, including furniture, site (purchased by Ramsden from the Darlington trustees), and paving of Darlington Street. The school yard was levelled by miners working gratis during the strike of 1893. £106 of this sum was expended on Johnson Street School. Mrs. O. Burton gave £150 towards the cost of the Mission School.

The Independent Methodist Chapel, 1893

The Independent Methodists built their chapel in Primrose Street in 1893. It cost £850. Previous to this they had worshipped in a room in Markland's Buildings in the Square, for which they had paid an annual rent of £10. Their connexion began in the year 1889. In 1914 additional space was added to their prosperous Sunday school, and the chapel itself was enlarged in 1932 at a cost of £1,225. It will seat 400, and the school, has accommodation for 350.

The Welsh Baptist Chapel, 1894

The Welsh Baptists in Tyldesley were taken under the care of the English Baptists in Atherton until they were sufficiently strong enough to stand by themselves. In 1878 the Tyldesley Welsh Baptists had seceded from their compatriots, the Welsh Methodists, and for worship met together in a room over a shop in Elliott Street. In 1887 they rented the Temperance Hall, and in three years became so consolidated they they invited John Lewis to become their pastor. He stayed in Tyldesley, and in 1893 began the building of the chapel in Shuttle Street. John Hughes, son of one of the original founders, cut the first sod. A prominent family associated with this chapel was the Lloyd family; two of their sons, J. T. Lloyd and J. M. Lloyd, became ministers in America, where the Baptists cause is so strong.

Holy Family School, Boothstown, 1897

The growth of Boothstown made it evident that some spiritual and educational provision for the welfare of Catholics, who had, in the trail of industry come to live there, was more and more a clamant need. About 1894 a room was used near to the Tyldesley side of Boothstown for mass by Father Grobel, and sometimes celebrations were made in a house in the Orchard lent for the purpose. A census of about this time showed 200 Catholics in the near neighbourhood, and in 1895 a site was acquired for the erection of a school, which would for the present time serve also as a chapelry. In this way sprang into life the School of the Holy Family, which was opened May 12, 1897. Mary Esther Collins was first headteacher. She was succeeded in time by Ellen Green, who from 1907–48 served the school with quiet loyalty for 41 years, until her retirement, January 30, of the latter year. In 1924 adjacent land was purchased from the Bridgewater Estates for the building of a church to stand in compact association with the school and priest's house. This was completed by 1930, and to the year 1938 Father Blake was in charge of the new parish, which in the space of just over 30 years had grown strong enough to be independent. Father Gore followed, and after him Father Byrne in 1948. The Church of the Holy Family is built near to the historic hall of Chaddock, and its high elevation over-looks the brown expanses of Chat Moss.

Hidden Trespass, 1899

From about the year 1888 the colliers of Tyldesley Coal Co. Ltd. broke through the limits of their concessionary lease under the fields at the bottom of Well Street and extracted a fair quantity of coal from beneath the Ormerod estate. The Astley and Tyldesley Coal Co. Ltd., were the lessees of the Ormerod minerals, and their miners tunnelling in the opposite direction following the rise of the seams stumbled through into the workings of the rival company, only to find all the coal gone. A long dispute began, which at first was arbitrated. All the facts were submitted to Alfred Hewlett, of Haseley Manor, Warwickshire, son of the vicar of Astley, who at that time as managing director of the Wigan Coal and Iron Co. Ltd., occupied a commanding position in the Lancashire coal trade. The Tyldesley Coal Company's defence was that the trespass was unknown until the plaintiffs discovered it. From Alfred Hewlett the dispute went to Herbert Asquith, then a rising Queen's Counsel, for his opinion as to legal liability. Failing to reach agreement the matter came up for trial in the High Court, where it was laid down that trespass, even though unknown to either party was a civil wrong. In December, 1899, the long dispute between the two companies was settled by the Tyldesley Coal Co. paying to the Astley and Tyldesley Coal Co. agreed damages of £3,000.

Astley Street Park, 1902

Tyldesley Council, desirous of laying out a park, acquired from G. T. B. Ormerod, at a rent of £10, a plot of land in Astley Street. This they extended in 1897 to Well Street by acquisition of an existing lease made in 1786 by Thomas Johnson to James Royle. Part of this land had been sublet on the south to build cottages and on the north to allow for the passage of the railway in 1863. To take over this leasehold interest cost £475. In 1902 the park was ready and William Eckersley was the person, who declared it henceforth accessible to the public. Four years later the bandstand was built. In time the park became too small and in 1916 Moss Meadow, then the cricket field, was added. This had been leased by Johnson in 1791 to Joseph Dean at an original rent of £12. 12s., the same long-term rent, which was charged to Royle. Then in 1927 the lessees' interest was bought out by the council for £800. The enlarged park extends to eight-and-a-half statute acres, the combined first rents of which amount to £25. 4s.

It was in Dean's field in 1802 where a giant oak tree, buried in the mossy soil, was dug out, proof of the pre-existence of oak forests on the Banks. Eight horses were yoked together to move this decayed monument of a past age.

Street Trams, October, 1902

An additional stimulus to the urbanisation of Tyldesley was the construction of a tramways system linking the town to Atherton, and through Atherton to Bolton and Leigh. This line was extended in April, 1905, from Milk Street to Boothstown, then later· to Swinton, where the Salford trams took passengers on to Manchester. The tram lines were placed in the centre of the road, single track, and loop systems were utilised to allow for passage in opposite directions. The economic life of these strange defunct conveyances was very short, and in August, 1931, the company responsible for operating them decided to substitute trolley and petrol buses on the routes covered by their statutory powers. The period of utility of these old trams barely exceeded a quarter of a century; at the end of that short period they had become obsolete and the patronage of a travelling public had transferred its favour to a more elastic mode of inter-town travel.

The Vicarage at Tyldesley, 1902

Ivy Cottage, opposite the present vicarage, was the house where the first curate lived. Its rateable value in 1838 was £15. 7s. 6d. The second vicar, Richards, was living at Fulwell in 1854 and later at Bank House. Then he went outside his parish to the vicarage of St. Annes, Hindsford, in Lodge Lane, and here lived Lund. In 1896 George T. B. Ormerod offered a site, and when Henry Mere Ormerod died two years later, he gave £500 towards a new and more con-

110

venient house for the vicar. William Ramsden added £150 and soon the present vicarage was in course of erection. Cockers of Walkden were the contractors. The paving of the streets round the new house was an extra item, which cost £268.

The School in Upper George Street, 1902

In the nineties of the last century it was recognised that the parish church in Tyldesley could not provide an elementary education for every child that turned to it for help within the township. The task was too great. The trustees of Top Chapel rose to the occasion by building a new day school in order to take off the strain on the church schools. The Rev. G. T. B. Ormerod gave an appropriate, convenient site in Upper George Street, and on June 29, 1901, Charles Eckersley laid the foundation stone. A day school had been attached to this chapel in early days, and Hannah France, Miss Atkin, and Betsy C. Smethurst, teaching in 1853, are among those pioneers whose names have been remembered. The cost of the building was met by public subscriptions raised in the name of the chapel congregation. In its early days the school was known as the British school. Later it became a council school, but the chapel continued to receive a yearly rent. George Beddow, a native of Pembrokeshire, was the first headmaster; he retired in 1926. Afterwards the school was subject to a deal of reorganisation and the elder boys were transferred to Garratt Hall School and the senior girls to Lower Elliott Street. It is now a junior mixed school. Thomas Aspinall was head to the year of his death in 1943; he was succeeded by Harry Latham.

The Church House, 1905

A Church House was first planned in 1901 and a list of sub-scriptions opened. Money came in slowly and William Ramsden gave £150 to speed the project up. The Ormerods generously gave the site in Lemon Street, and Joseph Ramsden, as his father was dead, laid the foundation stone. Its original cost was computed at £1,800, but this was exceeded. The building was ready by 1905 and R. J. Clegg opened it. Herbert Wallwork was its secretary to the year 1914, when he was succeeded by Ben Pearson. In its first year the house made a profit of £30. Trouble arose in 1925 with vicar Fleming over the right, which he claimed for the incumbent, to be a trustee. A committee was set up to oppose him and both sides were legally represented, when the dispute was referred for arbitration to the Bishop of Manchester. The day went against Fleming, and since 1928 the church house has ceased to be a useful adjunct of the parish church, and has been managed by an independent committee. A gymnasium was originally attached to the house and in 1908 the members gave a fine display before William Eckersley, of Lime House, Lowton.

111

Boteler Schools Rents, 1906

In September, 1906, the Charity Commissioners reported that £603. 10s. 5d. was paid to the master and scholars of the Boteler school at Warrington out of their lands in Tyldesley. This sum was a tremendous appreciation on the £3. 13s. 4d. original lease in 1526. It was made as follows:

Property	Area	Lessees	£	s.	d.
Cottages and land.	32a. 1r. 36p.	John Orme's reps	75	0	0
Cottages and land.	18a. 2r. 17p.	E. & H. W. Makin	60	0	0
Land.................	17a. 0r. 34p.	Walter Bannister	27	0	0
Land.................	1020 sq. yds.	Mrs. M. A. Hampson.	8	10	0
Land.................	5367 sq. yds.	Dr. A. J. Lowe	38	13	10
Land.................	1832 sq. yds.	Walkden Provincial Ind. Co-op. Soc.	15	0	0
Land.................	2002 sq. yds.	Walter Bannister	16	2	8
Land.................	1526 sq. yds.	James Cooke	11	2	6
Land.................	1a. 1r. 19p.	Dr. A. J. Lowe	3	0	0
Land.................	3062 sq. yds.	Dr. A. J. Lowe *14		0	0
		Mosley Common school trustees	0	4	1
Trespass Rent.......		James Cooke	1	0	0
Mineral rent per annum.		Earl of Ellesmere .....†350		0	0

* After 11 years increased to £24 per annum.

† Minimum rent.

The Labour Party Club, 1910

The Labour party began to show signs of apparent growth in Tyldesley at the beginning of this century, and the new social ideas found a more ready acceptance with the spinners rather than with the colliers. At the election of 1910 Greenall, the first of the Labour parliamentary candidates polled 3,268 votes. Soon after the election, encouraged by this disclosure of the ballot box, steps were taken at a meeting in the Miners' Hall to form a Labour Club. Councillor George Brown was in the chair, and the outcome was the purchase of Kershaw's clog shop in Elliott Street. Here was established the Labour Club, the first within the parliamentary division of Leigh. From this modest start many promising things flowed, and a resolution urging a national minimum wage for miners originated at the Tyldesley club. This was fought by way of a great strike to a success-ful concession. At the 1922 election Harry Twist was the Labour nominee; he won the seat by an easy majority and thus became the first Labour party member for the Leigh division.

A Board School, 1913

Agitation by dissenters, who objected to their children attending schools controlled by the established church, the failure by that church to provide adequate facilities for all the boys and girls of a populous township were factors, which, acting in combination, produced the first board school in Tyldesley. The site chosen was Barlow House in Lower Elliott Street, where by 1913 an excellent new building for scholars in Tyldesley arose on the ruins of the old house of the industrial magnates. It was opened on April, 26, 1913, by Sir H. F. Hibbert. At the same time the Wesleyan school and the Primitive Methodist school were closed, and J. M. Ely transferred from the Wesleyan school to become first headteacher of the new school. He was succeeded by Herbert Leather, who taught here to the year 1935. Reorganisation and regrouping caused this school in Lower Elliott Street to become a senior school for girls, while for the boys entirely new premises near Garratt Hall were built. Doris J. Middleton of Newcastle-on-Tyne became first head, she left[1] in 1946 and was succeeded by Gertrude Barker.

The Sons of James Burton, 1913

James Burton had several sons; there was John, Oliver, Edward, James, and Fred, and a daughter Mary, who married Thomas Fletcher. John died in 1879. Like his father he was of an unassuming disposition. He bought in 1866 the Eaves Hall at Clitheroe and went to live there. He took little part in local affairs and had no interest in the mills. At his death, Edward came from Norbreck to live at the Hall, for John left no issue. Oliver was a collector of curios and acquired a chair which had once belonged to the learned Dr. Johnson. He purchased an estate at Gwaynynog in Denbigh, where his widow died in 1893. Oliver died ten years earlier. This Welsh property came into the possession of Fred, on whom the setting glory of the family shone. This younger son gave £1,000 in 1891 for the infants school at the Parish Church. He carried on the shrewd control of his father's mill and lived at Hopefield, Pendlebury: he was for many years treasurer of Salford Royal Hospital, to which he bequeathed £2,000. For a time he was High Sheriff of Denbigh. He closed his long life in 1913 at the great age of 86 and left two sons, John Frederick and Arthur, and a daughter, Mrs. Bowen Davies. James and Oliver Burton were both married in June, 1851. Oliver Burton was buried at Henllan in Denbigh, and his widow in 1887 defrayed the entire cost of reseating St. George's church.

113

The Sinking of the " Lusitania " May 7, 1915

The German submarine, which lurked in the Irish sea-approaches and sank this great ship of the Atlantic crossings, cut short the life of Fred Isherwood of Tyldesley. He was only 29; he was returning home from America to enlist in the defence of England in the war of 1914–18.

**CHARLES ECKERSLEY
OF FULWELL.
DIED 1919**

Charles Eckersley, 1919

Peter Eckersley, the father of Charles, came from an old Tyldesley family. The father crossed over to Ireland where he was manager of the Dublin and Drogheda Railway, and the son Charles was born at Clontarf. Later the father returned to Manchester, and in 1866 Caleb Wright offered him a partnership in Barnfield Mills. Charles the son had sailed to Australia, where he spent 10 years in Melbourne, but he was recalled to the old country, when his father entered local industry. In 1879 Wright retired from the mills and Charles became more and more actively responsible. In 1886 the total number of spindles was 20,000, by 1904 the number was 200,000. Charles remained on the board till 1904 when he was succeeded by his son William, who was made vice-chairman of the Combine. Charles Eckersley built a cotton mill in France, at Lille. The father Peter was a staunch Unitarian and preached in Lark Hill fields at Astley in the open air before the chapel there was built. The son Peter left a large legacy to this chapel endowment fund. Both father and sons were loyal supporters of Chowbent's famous chapel. The Wrights and Eckersleys were interallied by marriage. Caleb took for his second wife a sister of Peter and Frank, the son of Caleb married Charles's daughter, Annie. Charles died in 1919. His youngest son Walter predeceased him and the wife Jane died in 1920. Charles Eckersley was a Liberal: he held a seat on the local board for a time, and was the first representative of Tyldesley on the County Council. His great business responsibilities precluded him from taking an active part in local government.

114

Vicar Lund Preaches His Last Sermon, October 31, 1920

Posterity writes of John Lund as a great vicar. He was instituted in 1884 and retired in 1920. Lund came to Tyldesley as a vigorous young man, and problems of magnitude faced him almost at once. The population was growing; schools had to be built and the scope for welfare work was limitless. By his marriage in 1889 to Susan Ramsden, he allied himself to a local family of substance, whose resources he constantly tapped in many ways for the spiritual benefit of the parishioners. This was his great work. He restored the church and reseated it; he built the chancel; he remedied the defects of the churchyard; he enlarged the national school; he provided the mission and the mission schools and the new infants' school; he modernised Johnson Street school; he bought the advowson; he gave the parish a brand new vicarage and he erected the church house. To measure these achievements is impossible, for there is no unit of measurement. And all this stupendous building was additional to the ordinary everyday administration costs of a populous parish. Granted he had great support from the Ormerods, Bayleys, Kirkpatricks, Ramsdens, and Lord Lilford, and local companies, like Astley and Tyldesley Coal Co., but the great motive inspiration came from him. In 1895 he was providing for the full-time education of 1,083 boys and girls, at a time when the Wesleyans took 340 and the Primitive Methodists 183. No other body secular or denominational did anything at all and in spite of this atlantean load, the education board pressed him to find room for 234 scholars, when there was not a place for them anywhere in the township. By 1906 the church had spent over £14,000 on education in Tyldesley and the greater part of it was raised during Lund's incumbency. All this had meant a tremendous drive on the part of the vicar, church-wardens, and congregation, and the township at large was a liberal gainer. The Bishop of Manchester was aware of all this and in 1905, in recognition, he offered Lund a better living. But the vicar refused and stated that he was prepared to make Tyldesley his life's vineyard. After 36 years he retired in 1920 and went to live in Westmorland, where he died at Milnthorpe, March 8, 1924. His wife died December 6 of the following year.

A House for the Curate, 1920

The curates at Tyldesley had proved a valuable source of auxiliary help in parochial work, and the Oliver Burton bequest of 1883 was specially marked as an endowment, the income of which was to go towards their financial support. There was an assistant curate as early as 1849; his name was S. Haworth, then in 1873 occurs T. W. Greenall, and in 1875 H. Edge. In 1884 R. Willett came to Tyldesley and left in 1894; on the occasion of his leaving a purse of 50 guineas was presented to him. W. L. Cottrell followed him; he stayed to the year 1903, when W. J. Gardner came. The opening of the Mission created the need of a second curate. H. Stones was appointed about 1899, and left in 1913. He lived in Johnson Street, and Gardner in King William Street. The latter left Tyldesley in 1909, and for a time L. Argyle and J. Earnshaw helped in the arduous work of the parish. The stipend of the curate was then almost £200. Some of the curates were married men and in need of a house. Willett, during his Tyldesley stay lived at 239, Elliott Street. In the year 1920 a house in Upper George Street was purchased from John Hargreaves for £600 and reserved for the accommodation of the acting curates of the parish of St. George.

William Eckersley, 1923

William Eckersley was Charles's eldest son; he was born at St. Kilda near Melbourne, while his younger brother, Peter, was born on board ship on the voyage home to the old country. As a boy William attended the churchyard grammar school in Leigh, later he transferred to Rossall School and at Manchester University intended to become a solicitor. But the father pressed him to take a share in the management of the Barnfield group; he eventually became a director and vice-chairman of the Fine Spinners. William left Tyldesley and bought Lime House, Lowton, as a residence, where he died in 1923. His brother, Peter, who lived at Fulwell, after the death of the father, died a bachelor in 1922. William married late in life, Eva M. Thorp; he left a son, Peter, and a daughter, Mary. In his leisure time he was an enthusastic cricketer; he founded the Tyldesley Cricket Club and was its captain for 25 years. His son, Peter, inherited the love of the game from his father.

The Vicar's Stipend, 1924

The church at Tyldesley coming comparatively late in history was never rich in endowments. The value of the living in vicar Richardson's days was £215. One source of this income has perished completely, for a part of the stipend in the old days came from pew rents. When Lund was vicar the value was about £300, of which in 1913 the pews accounted for £56. 11s. 3d. It became more and more patent that in time church sittings would have to be unappropriated, for the reform was forced on by a vigorous growth of new social ideas from the outside. The movement to free the pews began under Lund, and at the end of his incumbency, only the righthand block of nave seats was rented. By 1923 some 576 out of 814 were returned free. With the advent of Fleming the

the Ecclestiastical Commissioners promised in augmentation of the benefice a capital sum of £700, if the parish would raise a similar sum. This was collected in 1924, and the income accordingly increased by £63. In 1948 the whole of the church was freed from the stigma of rented seats, and to offset the loss of revenue the ecclesiastical commissioners made increased grants. The value of the living is now returned at £500, made up as follows: Queen Anne Bounty and Ecclesiastical Commissioners, £423; from minor sources, £44; from fees, £18; and from Easter offerings, £16.

George Ormerod at Tyldesley, 1926

St. George's Church in 1925 celebrated its hundredth year of existence, and to mark the passage of its first century the sanctuary was panelled. A descendant of George Ormerod, the historian, was invited to unveil. This he did on Sunday, October 10, 1926, when he spoke of the associations of his family with Tyldesley and addressed a crowded house from the chancel steps. His name was George M. Ormerod, then the living link bridging the great past and the uncertain fate of the future. He spoke of his ancestor, Thomas Johnson, and the great antiquarian, George Ormerod, who himself was present at the dedication in 1825. This same descendant in 1936 donated the chain of office to be worn by chairmen of the Tyldesley Council. He died the same year and the formal presentation was made by his son, George, who was killed in the battle of Normandy, 1944.

The Colossal Failure of 1926

In the post-war boom of 1919 and 1920 a set of unscrupulous promoters refloated the firm of James Burton and Sons. Only six years later this spurious company was completely bankrupt. The once prosperous mills, which had brought such increase of wealth and population to the township of Tyldesley were sold for scrap and razed brick by brick to the ground. The deficiency proved by the creditors was £545,000. In 1913 Fred Burton had died a virtual millionaire; only 13 years later, these mills, vast memorials to the sagacity of his father, had ceased for ever to hum and spin.

A Tea Planter Dies at Marseilles, 1934

Caleb Wright's son, Frank Thurlow, did not follow his father into the cotton trade; in contrast he emigrated to Ceylon, where at Wattegama he managed the tea and rubber plantations of the Gaphele Company. In 1934 he was on the return voyage home, when he took ill and died at Marseilles.

117

Jubilee Bungalows, 1935

Fulwell, that home of the great industrial magnates, became the property of a local mining company, the Manchester Collieries, and to commemorate in a practical way the jubilee accession of King George V, the old house was demolished and in its place were built eight bungalows. These were to be reserved for the veterans of the mining industry, who must at least have had 30 years' service and whose circumstances would justify the granting of a tenancy. Only a nominal rent of 6d. per week is charged.

Garratt Hall Boys' School, 1935

A new school built at a cost of £23,000 was first ready in 1935. Sir William Ray, M.P., for Richmond, was, in view of his local associations with Tyldesley accorded the honour of declaring the building open. Herbert Leather was the first headteacher, who came from the Lower Elliott Street School. Since 1946 R. Southworth has been headmaster.

A Scientist Dies on Pillar Rock, June 12, 1935

One of the many scholars of Tyldesley who went to the universities was Frank Roberts of Elliott Street. He became master of science at Manchester University and was an assistant lecturer there. He derived his enthusiasm for mountain climbing from his old mathematics master at Leigh Grammar School, J. H. Doughty. On June 12, 1935, Roberts died as a result of a fall on Pillar Rock in the Lakeland Range at the age of 31.

Wellington and Nelson Pits, 1939

These two small single shaft collieries were sunk by William Ramsden. The Wellington Pit was named in honour of Robert Wellington, the husband of Charlotte Fletcher, the owner of Shakerley, whose marriage took place in 1866. The Nelson was sunk soon after and given its name, as if its sister pit had been called after the Iron Duke. A man called Butcher committed suicide at the Nelson and locally it was often known as Butcher Pit. It stood near the old toll bar. With the amalgamation of local collieries in 1934 these two pits became merged in the group known then as Manchester Collieries. Joseph Ramsden, William's son was made chairman of the new combine. The Nelson Pit was worked out and demolished June 30, 1939.

The Break Up of the Shakerley Estate, 1951

The Corries, by marriage with Charlotte Ann, heiress of the Fletchers, added Shakerley to their possessions and in 1951 the then beneficial owner, Thomas Fletcher Malcolm Corrie of Stansty Park, Wrexham, sold most of his real interests in the subtownship. The farms—Greenfield, Oliver Fold, Common Fold, and Old Shams, were bought by individual purchase, and Tyldesley Council acquired Shakerley Common, additional to the land they had taken for housing by compulsory powers in 1946. During the period of Corrie tenure 1836–1951 several old land marks had gone and the familiar features of a former landscape had been altered unrecognisably by the spoil heaps of collieries and the filling up of part of the primeval cloughs. Pilwood, Old Nathans, and Guest Fold were casualties of this great change and Crow Bank was soon to follow. Eckersley Fold, Higher Oak, and Old Farmers had lost their fields and were now houses with stray outbuildings. At a later date Tyldesley Council bought Shakerley New Hall and Mount Pleasant. The ancient manor, Shakerley Old Hall, and Lower Oak House alone remained part of that once compact estate of 514 statute acres, made so historic by the records of every century.

Samuel James Fleming, 1952

The vicar who succeeded Lund had no easy task, for it meant that if the high rate of excellency was to be maintained, the new parson needed both wealth and wealthy support. Tyldesley as a benefice was not likely to attract such a type. The parishioners in 1920 asked the bishop to appoint the curate C. Bridge, but he refused. It was offered to the vicar of Garstang, T. H. Florence, who turned it down. Then the bishop selected the vicar of Denshaw, Samuel James Fleming. Very soon there was trouble and opposition, with the inevitable result of persistent ebb and fall from the high level of the days of Lund. Fleming was of Irish stock and was easily roused. He quarrelled with everybody and every organisation. He disbanded the G.F.S., he had differences with his organist, with the young men, with the Church House, with the Town Council, with the local press, with the Mission, and with the bellringers. The dispute over the Church House lasted many years; the quarrel was finally put before the diocesan, William Temple, later Archbishop of Canterbury, who in two out of three matters flatly decided against Fleming. But in one respect he deserved praise and credit. He put up a great fight to save the church schools and realising that to build new premises to keep all the scholars was quite beyond the financial strength of his parish, he wisely decided to modernise his present buildings and accept them as a school designed for juniors. This he had accomplished in face of many difficulties by February, 1935, at a cost of £5,013. In 1948 he retired and died at Wilby near Norwich in 1952.

Conclusion, 1953

The 19th c. was an epoch in Tyldesley, so great that by its record alone in population, trade, and industry, it made unconsciously a challenge of achievement by which other ages stand to be assessed. During the 20th c. the town has held its own by consolidating and improving on the heritage of preceding generations. What is known of the history of Tyldesley covers some 800 years, a period slight compared with time that was and is to be. Yet the lesson and challenge of the past is constant and inescapable: it rings out in the clearest of silver tones: the township of Tyldesley must in the ever onward course of time, progress.